The Soccer Syndrome

By John Moynihan

The author interviewing Sir Alf Ramsey on a train. The England
manager insisted on the lights being dimmed so as not to be
recognised and to ensure privacy. Cartoon by Nicholas Garland.

*For my daughter Candy, my family
and all Chelsea footballers.*

First published in 1966 by McGibbon and Kee.
Second edition published in 1987 by Simon and Schuster Ltd.
Third edition published by Floodlit Dreams Ltd 2015.

A CIP catalogue record for this book is available from the British Library.

ISBN 978-0992658540

Floodlit Dreams Ltd
5-6 George St
St Albans
Herts AL3 4ER

www.floodlitdreams.com

Cover designed by Alex Ridley and Mike McMonagle.
Front cover: Stamp Design © Royal Mail Group Ltd (1966).
Back cover picture: Action Images.
Typeset by Peloton Publishing.

Contents

Foreword

By Patrick Barclay

A review of the salient memories of four decades spent following football for a living invariably leads back to John Moynihan and the end of a long night by the Guadalquivir river in Seville. It was the long night in 1982 on which Scotland had taken the adventurous step of scoring first in a World Cup match against Brazil and their supporters had derived something akin to pleasure from the sound beating that followed. It was not masochism they encountered, more a pride in the quality of not only a couple of the shots that had drifted past Alan Rough – chips from Zico and Eder had seemed almost to paralyse the poor goalkeeper – but the general nature of their favourites' superiors. When Brazil eventually left that World Cup, punctured by Paolo Rossi and an Italy who were burgeoning into true champions, there was a sadness that sheer style had been found wanting and Scotland was but one of many countries thus affected by Tele Santana's beautiful team.

Our night in Seville, though, was two weeks earlier and all about the joy of football. The Rio Grande restaurant, with its terrace overlooking the broad water, was warm and lovely and held the sort of people who would be happy to discuss the game all night, as we did. The only one whose image remains clear, perhaps because the status conferred by his having been the first British footballer to lay hands on the trophy awarded to the club champions of Europe, was Billy McNeill, captain of Celtic's Lisbon Lions. Maybe, too, the quantity of red wine – not that there was a shortage of white, while rosado and cava stood ever ready to play their part in the gaiety of the occasion – contributed to an unawareness of whether John was still by my side as dawn marked out the road home and an unforgettable sight confronted the bleary traveller.

Along the towpath a group of perhaps a dozen young men approached. About half wore the yellow and blue of Brazil and half the navy, tartan and tammies of the Scots. There was nothing unusual about that, for across the city before, after and even during the match such scenes had vividly illustrated the atmosphere of one of those occasions on which football and friendship appear inextricably linked. But, when they came closer, a detail became evident. The faces under the tammies were swarthy and the arms in short yellow sleeves had freckles. The fans had swapped not just songs and bonhomie but their clothes.

John never forgot that night. It summarised his love of football and those drawn to it and every summer thereafter a postcard would arrive from Tuscany or the Algarve or wherever he was holidaying. On one side was a fine view and, on the other, always the same scrawled message: 'Not bad, eh? But not quite the Rio Grande.' We had become friends during the tournament, members of a group of journalists that might have been so bizarrely assorted in order to provide material for some of the essays you are about to read: the ones about what you would call coarse football, in which poets and painters would collude or collide with ruffians. There was, down the road from Malaga, the tall straight man from *The Times* who, despite the hours by the swimming-pool permitted by 1982 workloads – and even encouraged by the draw that had sent us, the so-called 'number twos', to Andalusia while the number ones covered England in the grittier Basque country – remained brilliant white. John and I wore sunglasses to protect ourselves from the glare of his skin. We marvelled at the man from another newspaper who recorded the quickest chat-up imaginable. Espying a German lady of a certain age as she slipped into the hotel pool near Malaga, he immersed himself in her wake and, by the time they had completed a second length abreast, had not only persuaded her to dine with him that evening but accepted a reciprocal invitation to go shark-fishing off Morocco later in the week. A more indolent fellow hardly left the pool at all, even to go to Jock Stein's press conferences an hour or so down the Costa del Sol; why should he bother when he was paying a Scottish reporter a crafty fiver a day to ring through with all news, 'quotes' and gossip, to be repackaged and phoned back to England with minimal interference to the day's sunbathing?

These were the slightly Runyonesque times of our lives, and John eyed them with amusement. Just as a fine footballer in his maturity often seems to be surrounded by space in which to perform, John appeared to attract an environment of vivid humanity. In truth it was his ability to define the material in front of all our eyes – to see people as often hilarious caricatures of themselves – that made him the storyteller you are about to savour. But he was more than that, because what John alone could do was combine amateur whimsy with serious assessment of the professional game at its most rarefied level. In one of these essays you might read of a park game being called off by an officious warden, in the next a priceless description of the majesty of a teenage Pele's entry into the World Cup in 1958. Yet the juxtaposition somehow makes sense of those times in which we wondered what the hosting of a World Cup would bring. He reminds us that we all play the same game. Or did. Do we now? Has the ever-burgeoning wealth of elite players created invisibly gated communities so that we never see them walk the street, let alone have a pint in the Queens Elm, as John chronicles in his tale of Danny Blanchflower and other luminaries of the old King's Road? What we get, amid all the fun, is a unique album of snapshots of English football as it prepared for its moment of vindication in 1966.

John would rightly laugh at me for saying this, but *The Soccer Syndrome* stands at a crossroads in the English game's history.

The one at which the game turned north and, forgetting the return from war to an austerity in which people had been gladder than ever to swarm into stadiums for some entertainment, struck out with confidence towards modernity, colour, and eventually the naked capitalism of the increasingly televised Premier League. *The Syndrome* was published not long after the abolition of the maximum wage and John writes of the new phenomenon of 'players accustomed to financial finery… who could not remember the bombs'. He observed a rise of professionalism and tactical awareness through the prism of his own beloved Chelsea in the era of Tommy Docherty and, at the same time – in the same place – the blurring of football's relationship with show business, a process just as obvious in the pop-star status about to overwhelm George Best in Manchester. Jimmy Greaves was almost as famous, and Bobby Moore was about to be.

On the subject of Greaves, it's a little surprising for the twenty-first century reader to discover that John seems to share some of the reservations that, in a matter of months, were also to be instrumental in persuading Alf Ramsey to prefer Geoff Hurst and Roger Hunt for the matches that won the World Cup. 'He has not always compensated for his lack of work in midfield, especially for England.' Those were John's words before the World Cup, not Sir Alf's in retrospect. But then you remember that Greaves had forsaken Chelsea (initially for Milan, though he soon returned to England to join the Tottenham team who had just done the Double under Bill Nicholson). It's as well to be reminded that Johnny Haynes, who made so many of Greaves's goals for England – 'one of the hardest workers to wear an England shirt and perhaps one of the most misunderstood' – equally deserved the accolade of greatness. And the reader of today can learn so much about the greats of the past from the comparisons of the knights of the flanks, Stanley Matthews and Tom Finney. All of the old positions, including wing-half and inside-forward, are dealt with even as they become – at least nominally – obsolete.

But our thoughts keep turning to the national team under taciturn Alf. As John taps into his typewriter, he reflects on the recent booing of Alf's men by a Wembley crowd. This had been in February 1966 – just months before a different noise was to greet the 4-2 victory over West Germany on the same turf. The booing – 'an extraordinary state of affairs' – had been heard during a friendly defeat by the same Germans. It had passed its devastating verdict on Alf's new tactics, which had been to eschew the popular long ball into the goalmouth in favour of patient midfield build-ups. What's more, he had arranged the side in an odd formation: 4-3-3. What hope had he of doing the nation proud with that? And who better to expose the quirks of the funny old game than John Moynihan?

I. Twenty Years

A dirty, fuzzy-grey serpent of people slithers across the Trent Bridge in the rain; a serpent made of men, and men with women, and men with boys, all with one single desire – not to be a second late for the match between Nottingham Forest and Manchester United.

The human mass forms on the opposite side of the river from the stadium and moves forward in vigorous jerks across the bridge; don't try and stop them coming the other way, because they'll crunch into you and put you down. The match matters more to them than you. Luckily, I am walking with the same ambition and I'll spit in the eye of anybody who gets in my way, because I haven't much time to reach the game myself, so get out of the way fat man coming the other way.

On our left are the floodlight pylons growing into the rain like four Eiffel Towers on a misty Paris day, and on one side exposed, in a postage stamp of dots, is a bit of terrace crammed to the seams with faces.

With half an hour to go before the kick-off, the pace across the bridge quickens and men move forward flapping their arms in fear of being locked out of the Trent Bridge bowl and missing the game for which they have been waiting six days.

Some walk three abreast in step, others push their wives ahead of them, or shove their boys along muttering, 'Cum on, for bloody sake'. Others lag behind wheezing slightly, letting their shoulders droop into their mackintoshes and their caps drop over their eyes, as they stare down at their feet splashing puddles; others stick their chins out aggressively letting their backsides roll with the human tide. A policeman waves them on.

Red city buses have deposited them in droves on the other side and crawl back in the rain to the centre of Nottingham for more passengers. There'll be more and more. We are almost on the other side of the bridge now, and a crowd of United supporters begins to chant: 'Denis Law, Denis Law.' Law, the genius, is back after a month's suspension and the month is January and the year 1965. Law makes a crowd move faster, so do Manchester United. We bump into each other on the bridge, sometimes breaking into a run, mackintoshes flapping, women giggling; disorder taking over.

The scene is coloured grey-green and splashed with red; red scarves, red bobbles, red rattles, red cheeks, red socks, red for Nottingham forest, red for Manchester United, who will have to wear their other strip.

Below us on the Trent, two boats from a local rowing club drift apart. Two pairs of oarsmen row gently in practice, smooth and unhysterical and so different from the massed, ungainly movement on the bridge. There is hardly any suggestion of muscle-power as they glide along in their white vests, each pull taking them away down stream. Their strain is disguised, but not ours. We are the ungainly crowd. And part of it, plodding on, I think back to another rainy time which was 4 September 1946...

It was an evening at Chelsea Football ground and Manchester United were again involved, their first Football League match in London since the outbreak of war, and my first professional match as a spectator. Nineteen years on now and my feet are still getting sticky in rain puddles and the team I'm going to watch is still under the same manager, Matt Busby. That was the night at Stamford Bridge when they beat Chelsea 3-0 and when I got hooked on The Game and Chelsea.

This was the night when the first of Mr Busby's incredible

combinations was exposed in full battle-order to a London crowd; all their delightful, clearcut attacking movements in the rain, laid out on the damp pitch as a hint towards the future. I remember the sky all turgid and grumbling and saw for the first time Johnny Carey, that gay, powerful unspoilt Irishman, and Henry Cockburn, the wily, stocky left half, who would shortly win an England cap and many more, astutely organising their defence, not that defence was really necessary against Chelsea that evening; in the forward line, Delaney and Mitten, invidious on the wings, and Rowley and Pearson pounding in on goal. And nearest us, the solid Jack Crompton, standing, arms folded, in the United goal.

And seen for the first time, Stamford bridge, that quaint, ungainly bowl with the dripping wet greyhound track round the edges of the pitch, the great slug of immovable terracing on the popular side, and the advertising posters behind the far goal, and the old, rusty main stand on our right, filled with pale faces, and the new stand, incongruous on stilts lying over one corner flag; Stamford Bridge, home of Chelsea Football Club since 1905 and still standing there after Hitler's war.

We had walked down the Fulham Road that evening which wasn't the Fulham Road of today, with boutiques, coffee bars, and smooth dollies and smart, expensive little houses, but a battered dilapidated street with bomb sites and girls with dried milk eyes and emergency dairies lingering with rationed goods and faded Bistro posters on the walls and V.D. warnings ('A Shadow on your Future') and year-old election slogans ('Vote Attlee') and faded pubs where Dylan Thomas used to drink with the snotty and undernourished.

The men who walked down the Fulham Road that evening did not look the same as the men who were going over Trent Bridge nineteen years later. Many were soldiers waiting to be demobbed, their soggy, khaki berets perched high on their heads, W.D. property almost worn into their skin; while others, back in civilian life, drifted along in demob macks and

square brown trilbys, brims tilted like Alan Ladd in the movies.
Compared with the crowd crossing Trent Bridge, the crowd
looked ragged, utility clothes hanging from run down frames
and haircuts inevitably short back and sides. There was the
same urgency to reach the game – war had never been able to
stop that – but the spice of living well was nowhere to be seen.
It was a time when a Wimpole Street physician had written:

'Once it is realized that all our patients and friends, all
England in fact, are undernourished, we can get some grim
interest out of seeing how common are the symptoms of the
present pandemic deficiency disease.'

But Manchester United that evening by no means looked
under-nourished. It was not an easy time for footballers returning from military service who, while being fit, were not match-
fit. Chelsea had several players suffering in this way, but the
United combination in their long, flapping kit seemed already
geared to maximum fitness; the Busby magic already at work.

It was as if one had discovered Proust, Rembrandt or F.
Scott Fitzgerald for the first time, a formative experience which
never allowed any going back.

In my ignorance Manchester United that evening were
merely men in red shirts making a team in blue shirts called
Chelsea look very foolish indeed. There was one man in the
field I could recognize from newspaper photographs, the tall,
log-striding centre-forward of Chelsea who was called Tommy
Lawton, his greasy, oiled black hair with a middle parting, unruffled despite the rain. But this phenomenal athlete, England's
centre-forward then, did no more than put the ball constantly
over the bar.

Crompton, who is now Manchester United's trainer, quietly
stopped everything that Chelsea and Lawton fired at him that
evening, and when he punted the ball contemptuously down
field the men in the red shirts invariably took control and moved
easily on their opponents' goal. The ball went into the Chelsea
net three times that evening, from Rowley, Pearson and Mitten,

with the Chelsea goalkeeper, named W. H. Robertson, flopping ungainly on his face each time like a man being shot. I walked away from the stadium after the game irrevocably hooked, not on the winners, but on the losers.

I still wonder why soccer first attracted me, because at the time I was at an East Anglian rugby school, rebelling against compulsory games with weedy, unathletic desperation. Perhaps it was the commentary by Raymond Glendenning on the 1946 Derby County-Charlton Cup Final, that first took my fancy and sent me looking for more soccer; that extraordinary ministerial voice which moved from a bark to a gurgle into a squeak and back to a bark; 'AND STAMPS HAS SCORED!'

Or was it the window-cleaner at our house in Chelsea, who perched himself high to try and uncover the grime of windows of a house which had long been empty through the war, mumbling to himself praise of Chelsea, and then to me about the Moscow Dynamos game which he said was the greatest match he had ever seen, and the crowd the biggest ever? And if I wanted a fair old time I should go to Stamford Bridge, because even if I didn't I would get a good laugh out of Chelsea. He said that they were called Pensioners with a wonderful centre-forward called Lawton.

Or was it a fat boy, with mushroom-coloured eyes, called Ramage at my school, who sat opposite me in the huge dining hall which smelt of furniture polish, praising Ormston, the Stoke City outside left, whom he called 'wizard'? We sat eating our oily pilchards and Ramage raved about Ormston and his qualities. When I became a firm Chelsea supporter, Ormston always seemed to score against Chelsea and Ramage, who shocked our school by joining the Young Communist League after the Berlin Airlift, would dig me gently in the thigh with a compass, and crow: 'We in the North know how to play football.'

But the concrete was properly cemented on that September evening when I became a Chelsea fan and Lawton became the hero. The years that followed were often as agonizing and frustrating as a savage emotional break-up. Chelsea put me on the scaffold on unlimited occasions, a side of such reckless disposition that at times they seemed more like a household of characters from a nineteenth-century Russian novel. Their biographers ought to have been Gogol, during their first, erratic seasons after the war, Chekhov during their tragic semi-final defeats against Arsenal in 1950 and 1952 – when the sound of chopping wood was heard at Stamford Bridge – and Tolstoy to cover the days of war and peace which followed under Ted Drake and Tommy Docherty, in which the Championship was won in their jubilee year of 1955, and there followed years of laxity which brought second division football, the sacking of Drake, the rise of Docherty, the fiery Catholic Glaswegian, who has brought new methods and a modern approach to Stamford Bridge.

The 1946 mob could never have scored a goal like Chelsea's winning goal against Liverpool in the Third Round tie in January 1966, they could have gone on until they were eighty, trying collectively to score; it would never have come. It was Chelsea's finest goal since the war, a fine clutch by Bonetti in goal, a quick throw to Venables, on to Harris, to Tambling and then out to Graham on the right wing. And then that delicious centre which Tambling headed-in off the crossbar. Following Bonetti's throw and the subsequent build up, not one Liverpool player touched the ball, players who normally regard it as a sin to allow the opposition twenty yards of penetration without being banged off the ball.

This was football patterned by a new decade, a new professionalism by new tactics, played by new players accustomed to financial finery, by the owners of streamlined cars and washing machines and perky haircuts, by boys who could not remember the bombs, and to whom Cliff Bastin was an ancient mariner in crumbling text-books, and managed by a ruthless, almost pathological manager who came from a humble home in Glasgow, played as a relentless wing-half for Preston and Arsenal and came to Chelsea to pick up the bits and pieces.

Some of his decisions, and the public treatment of his players have been peculiar and debatable to say the least. 'A bit of a nut', they say about Tommy sometimes, particularly when he sent eighty Chelsea first team players home from Blackpool in 1965 when he caught them out of bed and on the town. But then, and more important, he has made Chelsea into a team rather than eleven enemies at a cocktail party, and he has done so by not being gentle. Yet the highest honours still elude them, only a fingertip away.

Stamford Bridge has changed under Docherty. There is an elegant new stand, with seats in the popular side where once we used to stand like sodden herons screaming abuse at big booters like Hugh Billington and Benny Jones, solid post-war forwards of Chelsea, who tried to break the net when the ball was passed to them but who were often guilty of planting it in the region of Olympia.

* * *

The war was over, and the atom bomb responsible for ending it was still regarded as something of a freakish joke like one of those balls which can bounce to the tops of the trees. It was a bomb that became cliché and was used eagerly by the editors of football club programmes. In a Chelsea programme of the era you could read snippets like: "If any intrepid airman is brave enough to stand up to the blast of 60,000 throats when the Pensioners start goalwards, he will see something which will make the atomic bomb look like an Xmas cracker."

Eager to forget the war, the crowds rolled up for the game which was one of the few amusements going at that mouldy, restricted time, and the crowds then were mountainous because there was no television or other distractions to stop them. They wedged themselves into the grounds suffocating and hollering and sweating and at the Bolton-Stoke cup tie of 1946, thirty-three people died when the barriers couldn't stand the strain any more.

The crowds were greedy for football and they were not as selective as they are now. Clubs in old pre-war strip playing football as if they were digging a difficult trench could count on a vast following. Chelsea played Charlton when they were both in the bottom half of the table, and 61,566 people filed obediently through the turnstiles. They wouldn't now.

But not all the football was corny; a lot of it was mag-isterial when played by Manchester United, Wolverhampton Wanderers, Blackpool and Newcastle, and it was strictly British. The foreigners at that time hardly figured, being part of that sad desert of humanity described as 'the starving people of Europe'. Stanley Matthews, Wilf Mannion and Tommy Lawton, Len Shackleton and Billy Steel were kings; Pele was five years old.

The era saw the rise of the two great managers, Matt Busby and Stanley Cullis, two men different in personality and manner and approach but both giants at their trade.

Busby, the former Manchester City and Scottish half-back, was to have the greater success. A quieter, less regimental per-son than Cullis, he was, with his essential policy of scientific skill rather than brute strength, to create three masterly sides over twenty years. First, the side we have just met, who went on to win the F.A. Cup against Blackpool 4 – 2 in the greatest final since the War, then the gloomy side of youngsters he built in the fifties and many of whom died at Munich in 1958, in the air disaster which Matt himself survived; and finally the present side with Bobby Charlton, another Munich survivor, and Denis Law, the greatest footballer in Britain today and George Best, the mercurial Irishman with the Beatle haircut, whose team had their finest success when they beat Benfica in the European-Cup quarter-final in Lisbon in March 1966, by an unbelievable 5-1, a performance which Matt pronounced was the best performance by a United side since he took them over. Alas, they failed to repeat their form in the semi-final against Partizan Belgrade and were eliminated.

Matt is one of those dedicated, absolutely sure Scotsmen whom one feels could have been a top medical man, and in seeing him standing in the car park of a stadium before the kick-off, you feel a rare form of special confidence in the same way that one feels a sense of hero-worship for one's surgeon in hospital.

I once saw Matt standing in a bar in Amsterdam before the 1962 European Cup Final, having some drinks with friends. He was standing there quietly with a green trilby tucked on his head, and the Dutch puffing cigars in the bar didn't recognise him. I wanted to shout: 'This is Matt Busby, the greatest manager in the world.'

Stanley Cullis, the former England centre-half, the task-master, the boss full of chattering comment from the directors' box – 'Look at Broadbent, look at 'eeem.' A bald perfectionist prone to sulks, a dressing room tyrant, was the man who made Wolverhampton Wanderers into a great force of the late forties and fifties. They were a menace with their long ball during the era of Billy Wright, Jesse Pye, Jimmy Mullen and Johnny Hancocks. They crushed the opposition through fitness and speed and Cullis ranted and raved if they didn't.

But Cullis's success was not lasting like Busby's. Like so many managers he was sacked and Wolverhampton went down into the Second Division in 1965. After a bitter spell in the shadows he has now joined Birmingham City who are a very different side than the Wolverhampton squads. It was one of Mr Cullis' famous Wolves combinations that beat Honved 3–2, the streamlined Hungarian club side in 1954, which included Puskas, and Spartak, the Russian side.

These victories would cause considerably less fuss now – such is the improvement of our club sides in Europe. But at that time these were spectacular achievements, which brought howls of delight to admirers of English football. These sides were not unbeatable after all. Cullis could beat them with his long ball.

* * *

During the late forties, English football was in a cosy state, imagining the coming World Cup in Rio in 1950 as already won, and that playing would be a mere formality. But there were signs of disorder. Many of our internationals were now veterans. The Arsenal side which won their sixth Championship in 1948 under Tom Whittaker was rightly hailed for some superlative waspish larceny, inspired by the little Scot Jimmy Logie.

But this side, captained by Joe Mercer, was in the veteran stage as was England. We were seeing great things and gloating about our successes, but they were being done by men who would shortly retire.

A warning came on a November day in 1949, when a reorganized English team were torn to shreds by Italy in the diaphanous mist at White Hart Lane. Only a panther-like performance by Bert Williams, who had by now replaced Frank Swift in goal, stopped our side from losing. The white ball hit the net twice that day, both goals scored by England late in the second half. But the Italians in their economic blue strip, with Carapallese playing boogie-woogie with the ball on the left wing, had made England's defence creak hideously.

But it was still an era of distinguished English players. We went to Old Trafford, Highbury, Stamford Bridge and Deepdale and saw performances which made us croak with wonder. What more marvellous game could there be than Preston playing Blackpool, with Finney on one side and Matthews on the other?

The late forties were also notable for the presence and achievements of expatriates on the English football scene. Peter Doherty of Manchester City, Derby, Huddersfield and

Ireland made and scored goals of professional majesty. He was the Van Gogh of football, his red hair burning bright in the mist, who, like Mannion, provided academic lessons to our growing generation as necessary as a book of English grammar.

Doherty, playing in Derby's cup-winning team of 1946 against Charlton, designed a classic blue print with his other inside-forward partner, the silver-haired stylist, Raich Carter, which Jack Stamps, a rugged centre-forward, used to good effect to win the game in extra time.

And Doherty, rising late in the game to score Eire's equalizing goal at Goodison Park against England in 1947, and knocking himself out doing so. It is a picture which remains, Doherty inert, his green-shirted team-mates dancing a jig of joy as the Irish clan wailed with delight. Little Eire had held England, Swift, Wright, Lawton, Mannion and all.

And I remember a midget Scotsman – Chris Duffy, the chunky outside-left who scored Charlton's winning goal against Burnley in the 1947 Cup Final. The game was almost over when he volleyed in a terrific shot from the edge of the penalty box past Strong. The moment overwhelmed him and he turned and ran, the little fellow, long shorts flapping, the biggest smile you ever saw whacked across his chops, before falling into Jack Shreeve's loving arms on the half-way line. His other colleagues arrived for kissing a few seconds later, after a breathless chase.

Dominating the Irishman was of course Johnny Carey. When he led his side out onto the pitch, his balding cranium tinted at the sides with grey hairs, a sense of quiet authority showed itself in the casual way he flicked the ball onto the ground. And in his play was that subsequent quality of perfection, never hurried, never hysterical, always precise and the ball never booted in the tradition of a famous England and Arsenal back of the previous decade: Eddie Hapgood.

Billy Steel, who came to Derby from Morton for £15,500, a record transfer at that time, was one of the leading Scottish expatriates of the era, a dancing, industrious player who played with his hips. There were so many Scotsmen and they played with that efficiency and insatiable appetite for the ball which is their genre. Jimmy Logie of Arsenal, Billy Liddell of Liverpool, Alex Forbes of Arsenal, Johnny Harris of Chelsea, they all played as if they were making love to the ball. As hard as granite, all of them, but always utterly in control.

And there were smooth fiery Welshman as well: Ronnie Burgess of Tottenham, Ivor Powell of Queens Park Rangers, and Trevor Ford of Aston Villa and Sunderland, a rampaging, bustling leader. And John Charles would appear soon.

Some of these players represented Great Britain in the 1947 match against the rest of Europe at Hampden Park. Carey played for the Rest of Europe side, while Burgess, Steel and Vernon were in the British side. The full teams who squared up to each other on that lovely afternoon in May were, Great Britain: Swift, Hardwick, Hughes; Macaulay, Vernon, Burgess; Matthews, Mannion, Lawton, Steel, Liddell. Europe: Da Rui (France), Petersen (Denmark), Steffen (Switzerland); Carey (Ireland), Parola (Italy), Ludl (Czechoslovakia); Lemberects (Belgium), Gren (Sweden), Nordahl (Sweden), Wilkes (Holland), Praest (Denmark).

The result was a thorough 6–1 win for Great Britain, who, to counteract the close passing of the European side, concentrated on the long ball; the wing halves Burgess and Macaulay swinging the ball to the opposite wings. Mannion and Steel were too clever for the Europe defence and although Parola had a fine game in defence, he could not prevent Tommy Lawton scoring two of the goals.

Loud was the crowing. British football was seemingly invincible. So the Continentals returned to their countries with their heads hung low. And when they came back to play in club friendlies, the crowds here hooted with mirth and derision at the strange antics of the goalkeepers, who seemed to wait until the last second before flinging themselves at the ball, and they hooted with laughter at the strange gymnastics of the foreigners and their pathological reluctance to shoot.

John Harris, the Chelsea centre half, and present manager of Sheffield United, in his interesting little book at the time, *Improve Your Soccer*, formed his own conclusions about the failure of these European sides: 'I have frequently noticed a weakness shown by *most* Continental players and teams. They are so hidebound to what they have been told by their coach that they fail to use their own initiative. When something goes wrong with the scheme – when an opponent butts in to spoil it, for instance – they are stumped. The unorthodox plays a big part in winning matches.'

But the time was fast approaching when such statements became extinct. An army of talent was massing in Europe and South America, whose sheer genius – through using the word 'un-orthodox' – would soon rip our football to shreds.

The 1950s

The summer of 1950 was the time of the first killing. The English squad, looking gawky in ill-fitting blazers, and carrying wide, confident smiles on their fresh-faced, athletic young faces, journeyed to Rio with what we thought was a fine chance of winning the trophy.

But there was only disaster. When the news came through to England that our side had lost 0 – 1 to the United States in Belo Horizonte, men paled over their light ales at the unbelievable news. It was impossible, impossible, nausea set in.

But it happened, the United States, a team of unknown workers, popped a goal past Bert Williams and managed to hang on to the lead. And it happened because our players went into this game as if they were playing a village team. Well they were, almost.

A hasty reshuffle brought in the previously rejected Stanley Matthews to play in the vital game against Spain the following Sunday but although there was an improvement in that match,

Spain got the only goal and England were eliminated.

The trophy was won finally, much to the surprise of the favourites Brazil, by their opponents in the final, Uruguay. In the mood of the times, the English team returned without bothering to watch this final and showing the greatest reluctance to discuss their failure. The rot was setting in and Walter Winterbottom could no longer enjoy the luxury of a team which selected itself.

While it was a bad year for England, it was another good year for English club football. Portsmouth had emerged as a fine all-round club side with a hard, unpretentious half-back line of Schoular, Flewin and Dickinson; with Harris, a fast-raiding right winger, Reid, a dour goalscorer at inside right, and Jack Froggatt, who bashed his way along the left wing.

Big, solid and strong as a rhino, Jack Froggatt was later to move back to centre half for his club and England. But it was on the left wing where he crushed rival defences in the Championship side.

In 1948, Arsenal had gone to Fratton Park as reigning Champions, but the prospective champions lynched them with a superlative performance. In 1950, Portsmouth again won the Championship, but it was the Second Division champions who were by now acclaimed. Tottenham had lain dormant and forgotten in the Second Division since the War, but the arrival of Arthur Rowe as manager changed their history and laid the foundation of the smooth sides of the 1960s.

The push and run, or tip-tap side which won the Second Division Championship in 1950, and the First Division Championship in 1951, based their plan on team discipline. Each member of that side, who included Ted Ditchburn in goal, Alf Ramsey at right back, Bill Nicholson, the current manager of Tottenham, at right half, the captain Burgess, a shrewd reader of a game if ever there was one, and that whirling, interchanging forward line, of Walters, Bennett, Duquemin, Baily and Medley, were primed on a quick, simple formula of moving the ball quickly to an unmarked colleague.

It was superb to watch Baily, 'the ubiquitous and elusive Baily', as David Sylvester described him in the *Observer* at the time, and Medley, interchanged and interchanged but always so insidiously that you could hardly tell them apart as the two small, compact men danced through. They literally danced with the ball and they danced away after putting the ball in the net.

The side was never static. There was a new move which, unleashed for the first time, made philosophers like Professor Ayer mutter with delight in the stands at White Hart Lane.

It was clear, freshwater football; but like all great teams, it did not last. Rowe eventually had a nervous breakdown and Tottenham descended down hill. It was not until the new decade that they again became masters and perhaps even mightier.

There was the short corner to a waiting inside-forward who would push the ball back quickly to a wing half running in for a shot on the edge of the box, Medley's switches to the right wing to pick up a pass from Ramsey and the resultant ground pass across goal to Baily, Duquemin and Bennett racing in from the other flank. It was adventurous stuff, a new art, like Surrealism, having its specially defined period. This method has never been used as expressively since.

In 1951 and 1952, the predominant colour worn by an English side was the stark black-and-white, of Newcastle, 'the Magpies', captained by Joe Harvey, who came to Wembley twice to win the Cup, beating Blackpool 2–0 and Arsenal 1–0.

Their football was exhilarating, based essentially on flat-out attacking sallies. The ball was seldom swung backwards to a colleague. The team moved forward, always forward, as an attacking force like angry waves moving towards a beach.

In the centre Jackie Milburn and George Robledo were the spearheads with Walker, on the right wing, and Mitchell, a Scottish prince of dribble on the left, getting the ball through long direct service from Harvey and his mates in the rear.

It is difficult to forget Milburn's second goal against

Blackpool, a thundering twenty-yard drive, or Mitchell's dribbling against a very courageous Arsenal side, who had lost Barnes in the first half with a leg injury.

The North East saluted these wins with raucous enthusiasm. Somehow football had always seemed half to belong there, so suited to the mass enthusiasm of Tyneside, the salty shipyards where Newcastle, Sunderland, although far lesser forces now, have always been hailed as kings in the working men's clubs.

Two foreign internationals of 1951 gave a boost to England's sagging prestige. A coach from Aldershot took some of us, all pimples and in uniform, and loving our short freedom, to watch England play Argentina at Wembley. The game was notable for an extraordinary performance by the Argentine goalkeeper, Rugilo, a spectacular matador with a large moustache, who prevented England from scoring until Mortensen and Milburn squeezed two late goals past him to win the game.

The 100,000-Wembley crowd shouted 'England on' with almost unheard enthusiasm. They bellowed with delight and relief as we scored, but Rugilo could hardly control his tears.

Towards Christmas the famed Austrian side came to Wembley with their attacking centre-half Ernst Ocwirk. It was an interesting game, tactically finishing all square at 2–2. The English defence stood up well that day to the crafty Austrians. Nat Lofthouse headed a typically opportunist goal and Ramsey put in the other from a penalty.

Lofthouse, a bear of a man, from Bolton Wanderers, a former miner, appeared the obvious replacement for Tom Lawton, and one of his most notable moments came in the return game in Vienna the next year, when he scored England's winning goal late in the game. A bulldozing burst took him through the Austrian defence and as he poked the ball into the net he fell on the ground in agony after colliding with the Austrian goalkeeper. He knew the collision would come but he did not check. It was a centre-forward's goal and Lofthouse earned his title, 'The Lion of Vienna'.

But despite this win, England's time was running out and running out fast. Manchester United won the Football League Championship in 1952 but it was a side which still relied on some of its glorious veterans like Johnny Carey and Johnny Aston, who had moved from left-back to centre-forward. It would soon break up and Mr Busby would plump for youth.

Early in 1953 a spectacular sixth-round match between Arsenal and Blackpool might have been compared to a retrospective exhibition of late forties English football. On the Arsenal side were Mercer, Logie, Lionel Smith and Forbes, and Matthews, Taylor, Harry Johnston and Farm were out on the field for Blackpool. Arsenal wore unfamiliar blue and white shirts, which flapped heavily round their wrists and waists, their shorts were long and some of their players looked old. Certainly Blackpool made them look old with Brown and Perry a perpetual menace.

It was a good retrospective show with outdated kit and old masters predominant, and it was clear that day that Arsenal were cracking up this formation. Taylor leapt high in the air with delight as he put Blackpool ahead with a devastating shot past Kelsey ten minutes from the end. Logie equalized a minute later but Blackpool swung back from the kick-off and Brown nudged in the deciding goal. Behind the goal we heard the crack as Brown's left leg broke in two places. It was a moment of instant grandeur, followed by a moment of lasting torture. Brown did not play in the Cup Final at Wembley which Stanley Matthews won for Blackpool on his own devastating devices against Bolton a few weeks later.

This was Coronation year and the mood was right for England's national team to be in a juicy state. But, it wasn't; it was horrible, full of maggots and black bruises.

Shortly after Hillary and Tenzing scrambled onto the peak of Everest, and the Queen got a crown, the England football team, in contrast to all the pomp and splendor and general fervor of the moment, took a battering that was to be our most famous defeat.

The event came on 25 November 1953 at Wembley Stadium at the hands of Hungary. They destroyed us 6-3, mocked us, annihilated us. Our poor, incongruous team suffered, were shaken rigid in their long black pants flapping against their knee caps, their heavy white shirts crackling with sweat which had been shaken off torsos who scrambled to stop Puskas, Bozsik, Hidegkuti and the rest.

The feelings of the moment, the sudden shock of recognition were nicely emphasized in Geoffrey Green's report in *The Times* the next morning: 'Yesterday by 4 o'clock on a grey winter's afternoon within the bowl of Wembley stadium the inevitable had happened. To those who had seen the shadows of the recent years creeping closer and closer there was perhaps no real surprise. England at last were beaten by the foreign invader on solid English soil. And it was to a great side from Hungary, the Olympic champions, that the final honour fell...'

And so it came to pass that the 4-2-4 system was born to English eyes, played on that afternoon with a zeal and efficiency that ripped the ancient, lumbering formation of England into bits and pieces. The rudiments were basically that Bozsik and Hidegkuti controlled the midfield while Kocsis with his head, and Puskas with his left foot, provide the deadly needle up front supported by their two wingers Czibor and Budai.

Such methods seem mildly old-fashioned now that the 4-2-4 formation has been played in so many forms, and with the 4-3-3 as an added scheme and teams going barmy with centre-forwards standing most of the game on their own goal line and wingers playing as full-backs. But the basic formula was unfolded on that November afternoon when the pigeons in the trees along Wembley Way cooed out a lament for Stanley Matthews, Harry Johnston, Mortensen, Billy Wright and the rest, as they slid sadly by – lost souls.

From then on English football fell into a Hungarian mania, but the lessons were slow in materializing. Football managers rapidly dressed their sides in more economic strip, which made some of their lusty athletes look like naked refugees shivering in the snow. Centre-forwards tried to play like Hidegkuti and got lost on their own penalty spot. There was an air of defeatism all the way from the Football Association headquarters to the most exposed crush barrier at Oldham. There was an unfounded rumour that Sir Stanley Rous was having his own chapel built at Lancaster Gate to pray in.

One of the few players to master the Hidegkuti, deep-lying centre-forward system with profit, was Don Revie of Manchester City. His crowning exhibition of the formula was against Birmingham in the 1956 Cup Final, when Manchester City won 3-1.

But during the months following the Hungarian disaster we could only learn through torture. Like true masochists, the England team journeyed to Budapest the following summer and were beaten 7-1. A writer, who later left Hungary during the revolution for the United States, told me about that game recently. 'We were amazed,' he said, 'when your team took the field. We had always thought of them as gods, masters of football. But they looked so old and jaded and their kit was laughable. We felt sorry for you.'

Naturally the England mob did not exactly enter the 1954 World Cup competition as cocky Trojans. We made no progress except to discover that we had a natural centre-half in Billy Wright. The final was won by West Germany with a shock 3-2 win over Hungary. But this competition was a moral victory for the Hungarians who had beaten Uruguay in a classic and Brazil in a roughhouse, but went into the final out of touch against minor opponents they had already slaughtered in an earlier stage of the competition. But football is a psychological game and you never know what a sudden reverse can do to a team who have control of a game.

Walter Winterbottom had his back to the wall. One wonders how many times he thought of the left foot of Puskas while examining his face before breakfast in the shaving mirror.

In 1955 the supporters of Chelsea were astounded and delighted when the club won the Football League Championship for the first time, in their jubilee year. Ted Drake, the former Arsenal and England centre-forward who had taken over as a manger in 1952, got off to a bad start when he sacked the Pensioner from the front of the club programme. The club had poor beginnings under him and hovered customarily down the League for months, and were almost relegated in 1953.

But gradually Roy Bentley, lethal at centre-forward, Eric Parsons, 'the rabbit' on the right wing, Frank Blunstone on the left, and a stout, often abusive defence in the rear, started on a winning run which really got up some steam by the spring of 1955. Chelsea supporters, unaccustomed to seeing Chelsea in such a glorious position snickered with delight, but their club's presence at the top of the League was hardly noticed because of a Fleet Street strike.

We who were journalists sat moodily in our offices, drew our wages and went off to Stamford Bridge to watch Chelsea play 'in camera'. The deciding game was against Sheffield Wednesday at Stamford Bridge and some of us, armed with bottles of champagne, waited for Chelsea to put on an exhibition of a lifetime.

But alas, although they won 3-0, it was a typical Chelsea exhibition, aimless and disorganized. Our champagne corks popped in silence. The Stamford Bridge crowd reacted to their new Champions as if they were watching a herd of cows returning to a farm at teatime. It was not until the referee blew his whistle that they suddenly realized that Chelsea had won the Championship. The crowd ambled across the football pitch and gave their team a cheer; it was a drunken night.

Strangely enough, in the Fulham Road, Chelsea's greatest game that season was one they lost. It was at Stamford bridge against Manchester United and United won it 6-5. There was a nutty excitement about the game.

Berry, the United right-winger, had one of those days when he walked past the opposition, particularly Chelsea's massive, often clumsy, left back, Willemse. Manchester United were handsomely ahead but then came drama; an amateur – one of the last of the successful amateurs, named Seamus O'Connell, from Bishops Auckland – scored a hat trick and almost saved the game for Chelsea near the end. It was his first game for the club.

A few months later Ted Drake did something which the club supporters could only assume was caused by a touch of 'Fulham Road malaria'. He put Roy Bentley on the transfer list with some other Championship players. Roy Bentley went to Fulham, but he would have served Chelsea a good deal better than some of Drake's later acquisitions.

Meanwhile the establishment of Johnny Haynes of Fulham in the England side with his beautiful, reverse passes, the perennial youth of Stanley Matthews, the rise of Duncan Edwards and of Tommy Taylor of Manchester United had brought a slight improvement to England's fortunes. Against Brazil at Wembley in 1956 we gained a notable victory by 4-2, although Brazil had still to discover their super team.

The mood of football began to change in England. There was more money in the country now and rationing had finally gone. The footballers themselves began to change. They seemed to be younger, more handsome with short haircuts and a show-business look about them. The old, flapping strip was fading away, players like Matthews and Finney looked more and more like members of an ancient but distinguished clique, although their football remained totally majestic.

The players as public entertainers continued to be appallingly paid. But as television brought more and more international football into the home and foreign internationals by jet travel made more and more of an impact, it seemed the fashion changers were Matt Busby's new Manchester United.

They matured in glorious shape about the time of the inglorious Suez Crisis. Britain's prestige as a nation was split down hill and, amid all the horrors of the Hungarian revolution which went with it, the fact that at last we had a new attractive football team was a welcome consolation. It was the Coronation in reverse.

This was a wonderful attacking side with the massive Midlander, Duncan Edward at left-half, bubbling Eddie Colman at right-half, and Berry, Taylor, Viollet and Pegg coming through with breakers of destruction in the forward line. There was rarely a dull moment watching them.

They attacked without mercy and scored goals without mercy. If they were behind they fought back and beat the opposition by sheer exuberance. If their lead was cut they came back and built up another lead which was this time insurmountable. They greeted their goals with outrageous enthusiasm throwing up their hands and leaping with delight.

Steadied in the rear by captain Roger Byrne, their speedy left-back with the Eddie Hapgood touch, the side burst through to win the Football League Championship in 1956 and 1957. They would have been the first side to win the Double as well, but in the final against Aston Villa in 1957 their goalkeeper Wood had his jaw fractured by a seemingly unnecessary charge by Peter McParland of Aston Villa.

McParland scored the two goals against ten men which won the game and said afterwards: 'I was annoyed at the thought of a goalkeeper going off in a cup final.' The next morning he was the most unpopular man in England for United then were sitting on a throne of national enthusiasm.

That spring they did well in the European Cup which they had entered despite opposition from the Football League, who had forbidden Chelsea to take part after they had won the Football League Championship in 1955. Chelsea had meekly withdrawn but Matt Busby not only defied this ancient body but also took his side through to the semi-finals at the first attempt.

It was probably the turning point in our football history, the time when our football became more emancipated and adapted to the challenge of foreign competition. In the semi-finals Manchester United were knocked out by Real Madrid, who were to win the trophy once again.

The second leg at Old Trafford was televised, and the balding, aristocratic Alfredo di Stefano and Raymond Kopa, the French-man with the Faubourg St Honoré haircut, were seen by many of us for the first time. Their fluency, their professional zest and tidiness and almost clinical approach to goal scoring emerged; it was like watching great actors for the first time. Real Madrid in their all-white strip were a better side than Manchester United. Reluctantly we had to acknowledge that. Now football was capturing the imagination in a wider field through television. More women were watching the game and more people were playing it.

Showbusiness infiltrated into football and players and actors and pop singers who had, ten years before looked as different as parrots from partridges, began to fraternize. The showbusiness people started their own football team and dressed in all-black strip. The players started going to showbusiness clubs and wearing clothes that Tommy Steele and Anthony Newley fancied.

The game was becoming smoother and smarter, more players had cars, actor Anthony Newley could be found naked under a shower at Highbury after a hard training session while singer Ronnie Carroll and Sean Connery could be found in the bath at Queens Park Rangers after a bit of lapping.

Professional players nodded their heads good naturedly and agreed to referee charity football matches put on by showbusiness teams. They modeled their haircuts on the stars while the stars less successfully tried to play football like them. The crowds turned up to these charity games in thousands and the stars responded as if they were on stage. Between goals

Ronnie Carroll, Sean Connery, Mike and Bernie Winters, Anthony Newley and others flashed their teeth at the crowd.

And then came a shattering blow. On their way back from Munich, after playing a European quarter-final match against Red Star, Belgrade, Manchester United's Elizabethan crashed in a snowstorm.

It was a highly publicized tragedy, and with reason. Men wept in the streets of Manchester. Well I remember how clammy my hands were after reading the agency report in the *Evening Standard* newsroom. Half the team were dead... Edwards, Jones, Colman, Taylor, Whelan, Byrne, Pegg, Bent.

The result was that Walter Winterbottom's side, which went to Sweden that summer for the World Cup was halved in strength. There was no Edwards, no Colman, no Taylor, and Charlton, who survived the disaster, was unwisely not included in the team.

But although England did well to hold Brazil 0–0, the eventual winners of the competition, lessons had still to be learnt and we failed to reach the quarter-finals. We stayed in hotels when we might have been in training camps far away from the cities, we lacked a sense of urgency.

But there was some consolation through a jolly, brave performance of Northern Ireland who battled into the quarter-finals. Their goalkeepers Harry Gregg, another Munich survivor, was in inspired form as were the two other goalkeepers from Britain – Jack Kelsey of Wales and Colin McDonald of England.

A time of sadness and dull lifelessness crept into the English game for the next year or two. Matt Busby set to work building a new side, Tom Finney besides Billy Wright, retired from the game, attendances went down and Walter Winterbottom continued to have problems with another home defeat by Sweden in 1959.

The 1960s

The new decade unleashed a wave of uncorkable hysteria in honour of Real Madrid. They came to Hampton Park, Glasgow, for the final of the European Cup and won it for the fifth time with a memorable display against Eintracht Frankfurt by 7–3.

Di Sefano and Puskas, who had taken over from Kopa, in this memorable forward line, put on a colossal performance supported by the wiggling Gento, which stunned those fortunate enough to be watching that May evening on their television sets. Men watching in bed-sitting rooms in their underpants and drinking a glass of raw Spanish red, threw their legs in ecstasy towards the ceiling as Di Stefano weaved his way through the Eintracht defence from the half line and calmly steered the ball into the net. He scored three goals, Puskas four. Eintracht struggled valiantly but this was the complete club performance.

What on earth could be done to stop a team with men like these? Our football seemed to be going underground as our national team offered little resistance against Spain in Madrid. The BBC graciously showed a run over of the Real Madrid match again and the mantle which the Hungarians and Brazilians had held as demi-gods was now taken over by the genius of Madrid.

Then Walter Winterbottom amazingly discovered a team, an English team, which clicked; and Billy Nicholson unfolded a gem wrapped in silver paper with the name of Tottenham Hotspur.

The 1960-61 season was one of delicious rejuvenation. Tottenham Hostpur won the double with giants like Dave MacKay, Cliff Jones, Bill Brown, Bobby Smith, and captain Danny Blanch-flower, more garrulous off the field, supplying the deep thinking in mid-field. It was a season when they smashed all opposition, won the League in a canter, and beat Leicester in the final 2-0 in a game lukewarm and anticlimactic.

England meanwhile had not only discovered a barbed-wire defence without holes, geared to 4-2-4, but also an attack of purpose and determination. The team that season was Springett, Armfield, McNeil; Robson, Swan, Flowers; Douglas, Greaves, Smith, Haynes and Charlton. Memorable victories were recorded against Spain at Wembley when Bobby Smith, mud-splattered and a big ivory-coloured grin sticking out through the gloom, scored two wonderful goals in the second half to help win the game 4-2, and the 9-3 mincing of Scotland at Wembley where a Scottish goalkeeper called Haffey let goals in as if he were toast-master ushering guests into a diplomatic party.

Robson and Haynes formed a perfect link in midfield, Smith bustled, battled and provided Jimmy Greaves with openings, the mercurial Charlton rolled all over the field as if he really wanted the ball.

Jimmy Greaves, who was still with Chelsea at the time, a shattering adventurer in an otherwise limp side, was in lethal form that season, but his form was disrupted when he went to Italy in 1961, signing for A.C. Milan for £85,000. Chelsea might have done themselves a good turn if they had kept Greaves awhile more, because only a few months later Greaves sadly left Italy, rather like a public schoolboy who has failed to settle in and is taken away by his parents.

He packed his 'tuck box' and came home to Tottenham Hotspur for £99,999 in time to help them into the Cup Final for the second time in succession, score an exquisite early goal against Burnley, who were a fine side at the time with the sweet science of Jimmy Adamson at right-half and Jimmy McIlroy, inside-left.

It was the season of European Cup football at White Hart Lane, with the crowd roaring "Glory, Glory Hallelujah" as Spurs shattered Gornik, Dukla and then did battle against Benfica in the semi-finals. The second game was a game of savage, emotional tension with Tottenham two goals behind after the first leg in Lisbon. Tottenham won 2-1, but they were unable to score the goals which would have sent them through, Mackay hitting the cross bar late in the game. The crowd massed that evening as if they meant to blow Benfica off the pitch into Tottenham High Road. But it didn't work. Benfica kept their heads and went on to the final against Real Madrid in Amsterdam.

What an attacking final it was. Real Madrid, ahead 3-1 early on through a Puskas hat trick, then pulled back by the athletic limbo of Eusebio and Coluna to lose 5-3. Thousands of Dutch-men on bicycles sailed back to Amsterdam that evening spluttering in praise of the team which had beaten Real Madrid at their own game.

My most vivid memory of that match was the great Alfredo di Stefano sitting in the goalmouth after Eusebio had scored a Benfica goal, his head hanging down towards his knees like a king who has been captured on the field of battle.

As for Tottenham they had learnt their lessons and these they carried into the European Cup Winners Cup next season. It was the last season when the double side appeared almost *en bloc* as a force and they beat Atletico Madrid in the final at Rotterdam. British club football had tasted international success at last.

But the previous summer brought only confusion and disappointment as the side which Walter Winterbottom had built up so promisingly gave an inspirited display in the World Cup in Chile. Again the lack of urgency was missing, Greaves fluttered about like a stray cage bird, the defence did loyally but the forwards, with the exception of Charlton, were pop guns. Gerry Hitchens who was playing in Italian league soccer, was brought in to replace Bobby Smith but he was lifeless, his arts hidden away in a drawer.

England lost in the quarter-finals against Brazil by 3-1 and Brazil, as expected, went on to beat Czechoslovakia in the final.

During 1961-62 a Suffolk team of unbelievable ordinariness, but of quite astonishing efficiency when it came to scoring goals, won the Football League Championship.

Ipswich, who had won the Second Division Championship the previous season, under Alf Ramsey's managership, duly won the Football League Championship amid Sam Wellerish East Anglian enthusiasm. Ted Philips, a tall gangling man with long legs, and Ray Crawford did most of the goal-scoring, thundering in massive shots into the cage, but finally it was Alf Ramsey's coaching which did the trick and the big wigs of the Football Association did not let it die.

Walter Winterbottom chucked it in and Alf Ramsey took over as the England manager to prepare the side for the 1966 World Cup. It was a task which nobody envied and Ramsey, a reticent man, soon came under fire. His relations with the Press were often cool. 'He behaves like a R.A.S.C. captain' was how one critic described him bitterly.

So far Ramsey's record has not been particularly pale, as has been proven with notable away successes against Czecho-slovakia, West Germany (twice) and Portugal. But the defeat by France in the European Nations Cup was a fiasco. And later our efforts in the Little World Cup game in Rio in 1964 was a nasty pill to swallow. Since then he has based his team round a solid defence of Banks, Cohen and Wilson; a terrier of a worker in Nobby Stiles of Manchester United at right-half; Maurice Norman, and now Jackie Charlton at centre-half; Bobby Moore, a Jaguar type left-half; and a fuller selection of forwards, including Alan Ball, a solid, chunky ball player from Blackpool, the under-rated schemer George Eastham of Arse-nal, Geoff Hurst, the West Ham opportunist, Terry Paine of Southampton, and a far less cynical Bobby Charlton.

The problem as ever has been Jimmy Greaves, who has let Ramsey down on a number of occasions and seems to miss the presence of his old Tottenham colleague Bobby Smith who drifted into decline after England's 2-1 victory against the Rest of the World in the Football Association Centenary match again at Wembley in October 1963. Smith was not only dropped by England but dropped and transferred to Brighton for only £5,000. 'Smithy' had one season in which he helped Brighton gain pro-motion from the Fourth Division but he put on weight and Brighton let him go to Southern League.

Smith's bustle had allowed Greaves openings against Continental defences and Ramsey's problem was to replace him. As Stan Cullis wrote in the *Daily Express*: 'Transfer Mr Ramsey into another football era and reflect how much heart searching he would have in deciding on alternatives for Stanley Matthews, Raich Carter, Tommy Lawton, Joe Mercer and Frank Swift.

'This is not a nostalgic cry for the good old days. I realize this country has produced modern players just as good as those post-war stars, but I think there are more question marks attached to the present-day pool of players than in the Lawton era.

'If you consider how many England players have worn the Number 9 jersey in the last two years you can appreciate Ramsey's dilemma. He stands or falls on his own judgment, not only in selecting his team but deciding on the tactics to be used.

'His next step is to convince his players that he has the right tactical set up. . .'

Alf Ramsey, the former Dagenham grocer's boy, stands to win a prestige fortune or lose all by July 1966, for England's performance will be judged by this. The policy of playing a 4-3-3 team which is more or less 'wingless' seems to be the fundamental, much-criticized plan, and the formation which dumbfounded Spain in Madrid in December 1965 was the key to his intentions. However, Spain did not have Suarez for that Madrid game and Suarez is as important to Spain as Pele. And as I write the 4-3-3 'wingless' set-up has gained a lot of critics. It was a failure against Poland.

Ramsey's cold, withdrawn expression, as impersonal and mysterious and vaguely hostile as a duty officer marching up to inspect a fire piquet, hides a burning fanaticism and surely a trace of anxiety.

If England get knocked out early he will surely return to another manager's chair, to sit alongside rakish, rustic directors as he is portrayed in team groups of Ipswich Town all over their Press Room.

If he succeeds he will be considered another Vittorio Pozzo who steered Italy to victory in the World Cup twice before the war. He will be fêted and wined and dined and toastmasters will call out his name as reverently as announcing a Vanderbilt.

Perhaps we of the press and all supporters of England would like rather more communication from him, and less of an attitude that the England side is his and his alone. It is not his alone. Haven't we waited long enough for a team to win this competition?

Ramsey is not always a man to arouse confidence in the task. Is he trying to build a team with or without Jimmy Greaves; is his plan a mere flash in the pan relying on hard workers, players like Roger Hunt and Nobby Stiles merely following the plough? England's team will have to be a team of eleven Rolls Royces, average runners will not do. And surely he must play at least one established winger?

On a train going north to Sheffield, Ramsey was the only other member of the restaurant car. As the landscape turned into the industrial tattoo of the North, Ramsey gazed out of the window at fields and factories, giving the waiter a slightly embarrassed smile when he was recognized. He was going to watch Sheffield Wednesday play Everton and the odds were that Temple, the Everton outside-left was his key figure that afternoon. Temple would not now seem to be part of his wingless plan but that time his speed and shooting power had put him in line for an England place.

I asked Mr Ramsey if it was indeed Temple he was going to see. He looked up at me as if I was mad. The coffee cups tinkled and tried to sprint across his table. He looked just as edgy. 'Could be,' he said in a slightly refined tone. 'Now, if you'll excuse me.' He rose and walked away towards his compartment. 'That's Alf Ramsey,' said the dining car attendant. 'I know,' I said.

Alf Ramsey, the shrewd enigma, the terror of the press, awaits his destiny. We may hope that he avoids the fate Dostoevsky describes for a losing gambler: 'When once anyone has started upon that road, it is like a man in a sledge flying down a snow mountain more and more swiftly . . .'

Since he took over the England side, however, our club football has achieved a renaissance as imposing as the Venetians. The foundations were laid with Jimmy Hill's successful campaign when leading the Players Union in winning the wages battle.

We are actually dominating European football. The minimum wage was abandoned and stars began being paid what they really deserved. The young Chelsea side in 1965, which reached the semi-final of the F.A. Cup, were able to earn an average of £100 a week through league position bonuses. The incentives to do well in European football were phenomenal. And the Football League who had held out for years, relented. And Joe Richards, the president, and secretary Alan Hardaker, whose statements about players salaries during this long drawn out battle were nothing less than imperialistic, climbed down. The empire had fallen.

The set-up was now streamlined, the players themselves, wearing their almost shocking strip, appeared before us as young tycoons. They arrived at the stadiums in cars where previously they had come by bus or tube, they dined in smart Chinese restaurants instead of caffs, they wore slick clothes and had haircuts like Perry Como and Jack Kennedy. They were as well groomed as male fashion models and their dressing rooms reeked of after-shave lotion.

But higher wages not unnaturally put some extra needle into the proceedings. Some of the play in the first half of the sixties was nauseating in its violence. Before, it had always seemed to be the Continentals who did the shirt pulling, spat in each other's eye and punched freely at each other's chins. Now we were doing it ourselves and the crunch could be heard all over England. In one ignominious match the referee removed the entire cast of the Leeds-Everton match until they cooled off.

The spectators responded themselves, and behavior round the pitches became almost barbaric. Crowds at Manchester United, Everton and Liverpool, renowned for their patriotism, became savages as well, stirred on by unruly elements with booze in their bellies. At Everton Bill Brown, the Tottenham goalkeeper was flabbergasted to find a dart lying in his goal-mouth, while at Griffin Park, Brentford, a fan went one better by hurling a dummy grenade into Chic Brodie's domain.

But there were consolations in plenty; the continued magnificence of Denis Law, despite two suspensions for dirty play, the exquisite performance of West Ham United in winning the European Cup Winners Cup at Wembley in May 1965 against Munich by 2-0, one of the finest matches ever seen at Wembley, and a display technically perfect.

Tottenham were fading and it was Liverpool, League champions of 1964, cup winners in 1965, who were establishing themselves more and more as the force. They were as vital to Merseyside as the new sound of this decade, the Beatles, and the sound of their own supporters massed on the Kop, like victory revelers in Times Square, sang, crowed, and worshipped their gods. It was 'God save our team', and 'Eee Aye Adeyo We're Off To See The Queen', in joyous contralto.

Liverpool, managed by a tough, shrewd Scot, Bill Shankly, have based their tactics on spiky defence linked by Gordon Milne, a muscular half-back with a flair for goals. Shankly is quite content to beat teams by one goal, to beat down the opposition by sheer strength. But the fact remains that Liverpool have a side so flexible that it is not unusual to see ten members of the team having a pot at the goal during the match. But the system is still defensive, in this era of defensive football. And while their play is not always aesthetic to watch, they get results.

Matt Busby, who completed twenty years at Old Trafford on 16 October 1965, acknowledged this in words at the time: 'The game is played at a faster rate these days with a defensive trend predominant.' But watching his side, at the moment you still see the great attacking motions which he put into practice after first building up a side from the bombshell of Old Trafford in 1945.

* * *

That is why the crowd crossing Trent Bridge on a January Saturday in 1965 moves so fast full of expectancy. They are a British football crowd and they respond always to Matt Busby's squad with unnatural, pent-up emotion. It is the same at Sheffield when United visit Hillsborough or Bramall Lane, and the pubs full up faster and the ale runs faster out of the pumps on the bar, and the barmaids wipe the sweat off their foreheads and push out another ten pints. It is the same down the Fulham Road, or Tottenham High Road or Finsbury Park when Matt brings his side to London, and the same in the North-East when they come to Newcastle or Sunderland and the same on Merseyside when they come to Anfield or Goodison Park. It is the same expectancy too when they come to Nottingham to play the Forest, and on this rainy day the crowd moves almost licking its lips. It is usually going to be a great game.

On into the giant car park where you can hear the giant hum of the waiting crowd and the chant of spectators. 'FOREST da da FOREST, da da da FOREST . . .'

When the players trot out there is Denis Law. He doesn't look any different after his layoff. He paces around like an impatient schoolboy, rolling the practice balls when they come to him as if he owned them all, but also as if they irritate him because he wants to get on with the match after his suspension.

When the match begins we sense that he is going to do something incredible soon, and he does. Alongside him is one of the new young giants of modern football, the smooth Irishman with an executive touch, George Best. It is Best who is fouled after a languid piece of conniving. Bobby Charlton takes the free kick which is pushed into the scarlet Forest defensive wall by Herd to Law. In that moment we see the work of a genius generating in the mud. He becomes a blur assailed by anxious, slithering opponents and there is the ball lying solidly in the Forest net.

Law raises his arm like a matador and salutes the crowd. Is this not why we watch football?

II. Stamford Bridge

I got up at dawn, dressed and tiptoed out of the house. The red streaks of early morning sky hung over the bombsite on the other side of the road like a gigantic mural in a dark museum.

Suddenly the sound of steps, tap tap tap, men moving forward down the Fulham Road, heads bent, sleepy eyed. We fell into a group but silence reigned apart from the sound of our shoes on the pavement, down past the Forum, past a dairy and the clink of milk bottles in the interior.

A cold early spring morning in March 1950, going down the Fulham Road to buy a ticket for the Arsenal-Chelsea Cup semi-final at White Hart Lane the following week. Up at dawn for a ticket which would be sold later that morning. Up at dawn, because this was a game that we were counting the hours to see, biting our nails and fearing the enemy from Finsbury Park. Up at dawn to buy our passes for a supreme contest.

As we passed the Redcliffe Arms, the crowd became denser. It could have been the afternoon of an ordinary match day, a special solemn intensity building up, the pace quickening over Stamford Bridge and, then, the queue.

The queue stretched from the turnstiles, coiling round into the Fulham Road and on towards Walham Green station. It stretched on and on and I began to wonder and fear if I would get a ticket. I found the tail and it grew quickly behind me.

Phosphorus-coloured, dawn faces in the queue became more familiar as daylight gathered strength. The ones up front, the real fanatics, had been camping out all night, but while they were picking and scratching at spots on their faces and aches in their crutches, we at least had come from our beds. A police horse passed nudging us against the railings, so close we could have shaken the beast's white tail. The policeman looked down at us without compassion.

About eight o'clock a man in front of me started to talk. He was a tall, dull-faced man with a jaw so narrow that it fell away like a precipice round the edge of his blue lips. He had already rolled a cigarette and the smoke puffed up into the air with his breath, coiling away through the railings of the hospital on our left. Tobacco was spread on his greasy mackintosh. He looked like a hundred others in the queue, with that brown trilby.

'If Chelsea lose next week, I'll put my head in a gas oven,' he suddenly said. It was an ideal way to start the morning, something to remind us of the agonies and tensions of the game ahead.

I imagined this man on his knees pressing that chinless jaw on the grill, turning on the taps, saying: 'You bastards, Arsenal, you bastards.' I could sniff the gas there in the early morning as the man went on talking to a change of youthful supporters around him.

'Chelsea can't lose. Look what they did to Manchester United. They'll slaughter 'em,' said one of the youths.

'They'll win all right,' said the gas man. 'I've been watching them since 1920 and this is their best. Gallacher, Wilson, Mills, you can have 'em, Bentley's the bloke. Now look at it this way, his speed and shot, he's got it. Leslie Compton won't see him. But I'm still telling you that if Chelsea lose I'll put my head in a gas oven.' His companions laughed.

Visions again of him on his knees offering a solemn last speech to the turkey stains in the oven about his hatred and humiliation at the hands of Swindin, Scott, Barnes; Forbes, Compton, L., Mercer (captain); Cox, Logie, Goring, Lewis, Compton D. Turning on the taps and saying through his nose: 'I hate the fucking lot of you.' Death in Wandsworth at 5.33 a.m.

Chelsea had announced they would start selling the tickets at 10, so we still had a long wait. Some of us read the Sunday newspapers and picked up the comments about Chelsea. There was a long piece by a writer in the *Sunday Dispatch*. 'What has happened to turn this famed team of brilliant individuals and great inconsistency into a side which are now being talked about instead of being merely laughed at. The answer is simply that Chelsea are now a team.'

The gas man picked on this. 'He's right. This is the best Chelsea side. Now look at those wing-halves. Armstrong's a worker and he's got class, Mitchell's a beauty. Look at the way they nailed Manchester, bloody nailed them.'

'What a goal,' said a youth offering us the grandeur of that moment.

We all knew about the goal, Bentley's shot from the edge of the Manchester United penalty box from Billy Gray's back-heel which roared up into the roof of Crompton's net with John Carey looking up speechless with horror. A youth behind me bit me in the neck after that goal to celebrate Chelsea's march in the semi-final. It was accidental but half meant, my neck having bounced into his jabbering mouth as the stadium erupted and men fainted away. It was my first love bite and there was blood on my blue and white scarf after the game.

'That goal, well bloody hell it was the best goal ever,' said the gas man. 'In like a bloody rocket. Crompton got a good smell of burning bleeding leather but that's all. Bloody marvellous.'

'Gently Bentley,' said a youth with blue eyes looking down at the pavement.

It was a popular expression lumbered on our centre-forward through the Jimmy Edwards-Dick Bentley show, 'Take it from Here'. Every time our centre-forward rose for the ball in a newspaper photograph the caption writers scribbled, 'Gently Bentley' into the text.

'Well he won't be gentle at White Hart Lane,' said the gas

man. 'Compton won't get near him. Les'll catch pneumonia out there from Roy's drought.'

'Gentley Bentley,' somebody else sniggered.

'Look at those geysers up the front of the queue,' said the gas man. 'Bet they missed getting up their old women last night. Didn't fancy the all night session meself. Had a few pints, got up the old woman and came down here with tea in me belly. We'll get a ticket here, you see. Nothing to worry about.'

One hour to wait before they started selling tickets. The queue had swelled out into the Fulham Road so that people were now standing along the centre of the road. The human mass remained static, pushed occasionally in a more solid jelly by the subtle wriggle of the police horse's backside.

The gas man had youth round him. He looked at us with sardonic acceptance nodding his head at some remark about Chelsea and then offering his own judgments in a loud, unlovely voice.

'What you think the score will be,' said a youth with a face like a weasel.

'Chelsea 3, Arsenal 0' He hung an 'o' in the morning air and is slowly drifted away. 'Roy'll put two in the net before Mercer's got his tits warm. Mitchell, Billy Gray, Roy and a goal, you'll see. Swindin will be lying there as if he's kicked the bucket with the ball in the net, you'll see.'

'What if they lose, what if they lose,' said the weasel youth.

'Then I'll put me bleeding head in a gas oven.'

We laughed. The gasman became dictatorial, his statements more and more lengthy. With Chelsea playing so well he did not oblige us with one criticism about the club although a year before he would probably have been verbally lynching Billy Birrell and his team for their disorders. But supporters are fickle and there is no criticism when their team is playing extremely well.

'Roy's a better centre-forward than Tommy Lawton,' said the gasman. 'He's got more guts. Lawton was a bighead. Roy gets on with the game and he moves around. He's a bloody marvel.'

The sun came out, first a feeble yellow glow, then brightening up into warm, orange rays; the queue shuffled forward an inch as if the changing weather itself had the power to open the gates of Chelsea Football Club and let us in.

When the gates did open we heard all about it. There were cheers ahead and rattles sounded off clanking in jets of noise.

'Up the Blues,' someone shouted.

'Up the Pensioners,' said the gas man.

'Gently Bentley,' said the youth.

We were moving up, shuffling up, jostling up the Fulham Road past dirty white studios on our left. Above them was the high, ever impending top of the Stamford Bridge terraces and the roof of the stand. People inside the studios were still asleep. One dissipated face with a touch of a beard looked at us from a bathroom window and then disappeared. He would have seen a monstrous crowd moving past, head to head, shoulder to shoulder, arm to arm, a masculine crowd with chins up high to see how far there was to go till the turnstiles.

We moved steadily past a man playing 'Music, Music, Music,' on an accordion, the current hit tune of that time. The pile of youths round us whistled in time: 'Put another nickel in…'

The gas man rolled along, his shoulders hunched round his chin. 'See you at Wembley, lads,' he said as we came up to the club gates where the mounted police were jostling the huge mass of people. 'See you at Wembley. They can't lose. It will be a Chelsea-Liverpool Cup Final, you see. And Johnny Harris'll be holding up the Cup.'

'What'll you do if they lose?' asked the youth with the weasel face.

'Put my head in the gas oven.'

A man in Wandsworth found dead at 5.33 a.m. leaving a note: 'I did this because the bleeders lost, my bleeders.' The sweet smell of death intermingled by gas. They found him a long time after. He wasn't married despite what he said in the queue.

We were up at the turnstiles and I bought a terrace ticket for the White Hart Lane tie, behind one of the goals. When I went through the gas man had disappeared. Going out of the ground I looked down the Fulham Road towards Walham Green but couldn't see much because of all the faces coming forward.

I walked home in time for Sunday lunch. My parents said it must have been boring to have to wait in the queue for so long. I told them about the man in the queue threatening to commit suicide and they laughed: 'Well, he'll probably be forced to do it. I can't see Chelsea winning,' said my father. He was right.

The story did not have a happy ending. Arsenal and Chelsea drew the first match, 2-2 and the tension was appalling. Roy Bentley did score early goals as the gas man predicted, the first a beautiful lob over Swindin's head, the second a glided header just inside the post. Standing behind the net with my blue and white scarf covered with blood and perspiration, I dreamt of Wembley and Bentley doing the same thing there.

Chelsea were ahead and so much ahead that they became lax against the weight of an Arsenal revival. A minute before half time Freddie Cox swung over an inswinging corner and it plopped into the Chelsea net. In the second half the torture was sealed when Leslie Compton headed in his brother's corner kick, a wave of Arsenal supporters invaded the pitch, and a replay was set for the following Wednesday.

Arsenal won that game in extra time against a Chelsea side weakened by injuries. The goal, again scored by Cox, the tormentor of Chelsea, could have been prevented by a more agile defence. I can still see the ball coming towards me, Medhurst diving, the ball tucking itself into the net and the Arsenal lot running onto the pitch bellowing with joy.

Freddie Cox told how he scored the goal to Desmond Hackett in the *Daily Express*: 'Young Pete (Goring) slipped me a peach of a pass as I stood on the edge of the penalty area. I could see the Chelsea defence lined up, five of them wondering what I was going to do. I wasn't so sure myself.

'Then I realized that Goring and Jimmy Logie were distracting the defence.'

'I moved along the line and I couldn't help thinking it was like an officer inspecting a parade. No one moved. I just went on and on. I couldn't believe it.

'Then I saw the goal and I let go with my "swinger" – the old left foot.

'I knew it was a goal. It seemed for a whole second that the game had suddenly stopped dead. The next thing I knew that Reg Lewis was holding me in his arms like a mother nursing a baby.'

So Arsenal went on to Wembley for the fifth time and eventually won the Cup, beating Liverpool 2-0. Chelsea moved into an era of decline. The night they lost that replay I remember coming home on the Piccadilly line and sitting miserably in our kitchen, eating a sausage and trying not to cry. I still wonder if the gasman killed himself at 5.33 a.m.

III. School

I went to a rugby school and hated the game. Buried in a steaming scrum, with my ears almost severed by the weighty hips of two second-row forwards, I stared at the grass below and, as a heel lashed into my nose, dreamt of the fruits of the outside world beyond the school gates.

In particular, the main apple was Association Football, an unmentionable code at our institution which burned with minor snobbery.

Three or four of us would take the *round* ball out on Sunday afternoon and boot it about hopefully between a pair of rugby posts and inevitably the master in charge of school rugby would appear with his walking stick and 1st XV scarf on the edge of the touch line, his retriever licking lovingly at his cavalry-twill trousers.

I remember the look of hatred he used to give us, although there was nothing he could do about it, except glare, as we were allowed in theory to kick a soccer ball about on Sundays. His moustache full of the cold cream he used to rub on to keep away a selection of nameless spots which grew up in the week during his classics classes, would spread over his cheeks as he pushed out his ample lips in agony and frustration. But we felt we were Frank Swift and Tommy Lawton and Stanley Mortensen and we took no notice of him.

Because soccer was not a polite word, we pressed on, educating ourselves from the outside with such 'Red Cross' gifts as the *Football Association Book for Boys*. During this era there was a figure in a soccer educational series we took to in these volumes named Mr. Winkle – 'the old school coach' – a father figure if ever there was one.

Mr. Wrinkle was a warm-hearted, inoffensive sort of man with a cap, a scarf, a long droopy moustache and a pipe which drooped out of the corners of his mouth. He had, like so many men similar, a repressed homosexual tendency which amounted to asking young admirers back to tea and letting them snuggle against his knee-caps by the fireside.

Mr. Wrinkle grew more and more indispensible to us, and when in later years I met the artist, Robert Hunt, who created his image, I was amazed by Hunt's lack of concern over the great game. Hunt, a good illustrator with long sideboards and a tendency to shout at parties, showed very little interest apart from saying he had gone to the Valley as a boy. The creator of Mr. Wrinkle turned out not to be a fanatic of the terraces but a bustling Bohemian with a love for straight Scotch rather than Mr. Wrinkle's constant recipe for a growing soccer player: lemonade.

But Mr. Hunt appeared much later in my life than Mr. Wrinkle, who was at one stage deeply necessary to me. Mr. Wrinkle's soul love was a small blonde boy with freckles called Dan. Dan sometimes seemed slightly frivolous and lacking in gratitude to all Mr. Wrinkle's intrinsic instructions.

He was a fickle hero of his school team and Mr. Wrinkle, wrapped up warmly against the cold of a northern winter, would plod out to watch his games. Mr. Wrinkle had something of a reputation as a footballer during the reign of Queen Victoria when he had played good class amateur football. We had seen drawings of him during this era wearing long flapping shirts done up at the point of the swollen Adam's Apple by a button, a huge club badge on his left nipple, a long pair of black shorts below his knees, a pair of boots which would have winded an elephant, and outside his socks a pair of shin pads the size of Norman shields.

He was full of memories and, after watching Dan play, standing the other side of the opposition's upright so he could view every flicker of Dan's perpetual industry, he would ask the young blond back to tea with some of his friends for advice.

Dan always came with alacrity because he was a perfectionist. At our rugby school we noted everything Mr. Wrinkle had to say, envying the way Dan was able to snuggle up against Mr. Wrinkle's knees for advice.

Mr. Wrinkle lived in a cosy, little Victorian house, in an inoffensive part of town and his hearthrug was one of the nicest places you could find at five thirty p.m. on a Saturday afternoon, with the cold mist coming down outside and the street lamps throwing out dingy, yellow beams.

Mr. Wrinkle would sit back and puff at his pipe while Dan and his friends lounged round the fireside drinking tea, eating endless cakes and looking at Mr. Wrinkle's scrap books.

One afternoon Dan came across a rather titanic photograph of a player in one of Mr. Wrinkle's albums, with a long black drooping moustache and black convict's haircut.

'Who is this chap with the moustache,' he asked Mr. Wrinkle who was leaning back in his chair idly scratching his still muscular thighs. Mr. Winkle sucked at his pipe which lolled from his mouth and starred up in silence for a moment towards the crackling fire. The boys looked up at him in wonder and waited for him to speak, but for a moment the great man was struck dumb with ecstasy.

Then he rose to his feet and the boys, out of politeness, followed suit allowing him to stand with his backside facing the hearth. Mr. Wrinkle then spoke in a mixture of North-country and Grammar School English. He said that the man with the moustache 'was Wotherspoon', his trusted right-winger, 'with a burst of speed as good as Meredith and a body swerve which Tom Finney would find it hard to equal now'.

'Wotherspoon once took a corner I'll never forget,' said Mr. Wrinkle. He stood against the fire, his pipe still drooping out of a corner of his mouth, a trace of tea hanging from his moustache and demonstrated how Wotherspoon had done it.

'I well remember how he looked for a point six to ten in front of the goal-post! – and the way he glued his eyes on the ball as he kicked it.' Mr. Wrinkle curled his right foot over an imaginary football and stared down hard at the carpet. 'And how his body leant back in the art of kicking.'

Dan crouched down at Mr. Wrinkle's feet and stared up at him licking his lips at the story. His friends stood round in respectful silence holding their hands clenched together. Mr. Wrinkle was getting more and more excited.

'The ball was placed in front of the goal-mouth, dropping just in front of myself...' There was a pause as he took a sip of tea and looked at the boys so as to give them time to absorb the story. He continued: 'Myself, who was playing centre-forward, saw an opening.' Mr. Wrinkle leaned forward aggressively and hit out towards the opposite wall with his left foot. 'It was an easy goal. But it was really Wotherspoon's kick which scored it.'

On these occasions Mr. Winkle was full of anecdotes which usually culminated in his hitting the ball into the net, although he modestly always illustrated with a touch of genius by a colleague.

The freckly Dan was not always able to do things as easily as Mr. Wrinkle by the fireside. He had certain neurotic tendencies, a certain raggedness when it came to approach, sloppiness near the goal. His whole playing outlook was fraught with problems and he leaned heavily on the father figure, Mr. Wrinkle, as an analyst after his bad games. Mr. Wrinkle gave him his fireside as couch and we young readers were allowed to observe the sessions. They usually had happy endings.

Dan sometimes went into a school game with deep forebodings. The school hero would lose his confidence early on and his colleagues, who relied on him to score last minute goals to win vital matches, would hang their heads and mutter at his sloppiness. There was nothing of the superman about

Dan. His vulnerability shone out in pathetic streaks on the
school playing fields. Mr. Wrinkle would stand on the touchline
running a pair of sad, almost senile eyes over his favourite and
trying to discover what was wrong.

Dan never got a scoulding from Mr. Wrinkle, which is
why we admired the old man so much. There were no Stanley
Cullis-roastings at the end of a bad performance. Only a warm,
affectionate squeeze which Mr. Wrinkle deposited round Dan's
muddy thighs with his hand.

In one disastrous game Dan's team were drawing 2–2
and the time was right for Dan to score the hero's goal. His
left-winger got away, out past the clumsy lunge of the opposing right-back and pulled back a perfect centre for Dan. The
boy rose high in the air as if pulled up by a kite but something
behind the goal, possibly the sight of Mr. Wrinkle sticking out
his chin in suspense, caused Dan to coyly shut his eyes and he
missed the centre altogether. The other team broke away and
scored the winning goal.

Dan was a picture of misery after the game and nobody
would speak to him. He shuffled out of the school gates into
the street and there hidden behind a lamppost breathing deeply
was Mr. Wrinkle wrapped up in winter woolens, his cap pulled
down over his ears so that the piece of hair jutting out at one
side looked absurd. He took Dan's arm and gave it a gentle
squeeze: 'Come and have some tea, Dan.'

The boy accepted with alacrity, sensing that only his analyst
or adviser, or rather Mr. Wrinkle could help him. He settled
down in Mr. Wrinkle's narrow little chair the old man usually
reserved for himself, while Mr. Wrinkle willingly took the hard
backed chair opposite. Dan's blue and white blazer stood out in
the cheerful room decorated with portraits of Mr. Wrinkle as
player, and his hands shook slightly as he held his teacup.

Mr. Wrinkle was less affectionate than usual. He took his
pipe out of his mouth and waved it earnestly towards Dan: 'I
saw it,' he said. Dan looked sad knowing that what Mr. Wrinkle

had seen was horrible. 'Keep your eyes on the ball, son. Practice on your own,' said Mr. Wrinkle dribbling slightly at the mouth.

They sat there for a long while eating crumpets and staring into the red embers of the fire and talking about the art of heading, until Mr. Wrinkle gave Dan a warm squeeze of the hand and said he would have to go home because he had to go out to get the classified football results edition.

Dan went away and that night began to practice by lamp-light in the back alleys of the semi-detached area where he lived. Other boys, who watched him thudding the ball with tons of neck muscle power against the wall and sending back the rebounds with his forehead as if he hated the sight of the ball, roared with laughter.

As we looked at Dan being laughed at we sympathized with him because we were used to being laughed at ourselves when we kicked a football. Dan's problems became our own.

Dan went on heading the ball against targets or walls all that next week and took no notice of the scorn thrown at him. Mr. Wrinkle's advice had become an obsession with him. At nights he dreamed of Mr. Wrinkle looming over him and telling him to head to the ball. Dan used to wake up soaked in sweat thrusting his head backwards and forwards. Unlike many other boys of his age group, he still had no masturbatory tendencies.

Came the big match the following week and Dan gleaming in his striped strip ran out onto the field full of confidence and anxious to do well. It went well for him. During the game he remembered Mr. Wrinkle's advice as the ball came over from a corner – 'Watch the ball until it hits.'

Dan got up high and kept his eyes open despite Mr. Wrinkle's presence again behind the goal. He no longer felt coy or shy and he headed the ball into the top left-hand corner of the net like a rocket. There was a great roar from his school supporters and his colleagues hugged him.

After the game Mr. Wrinkle intercepted Dan, who with childish enthusiasm for the moment and with that lack of gratefulness natural to the young, had almost cut the old man dead. Mr. Wrinkle had to throw out an arm and stop the lad from rushing past him. Dan stood there panting with pleasure, his freckles moving up and down in the red glow of evening. 'With practice, you can flick the ball wherever you want,' said Mr. Wrinkle.

Dan gave a brief nod and turned away to the dressing room. Mr. Wrinkle went home to tea, alone. He did not ask Dan back again until the lad had another bad game because he found him less bumptious on those occasions. But he was very fond of the lad in general. He would have to sort him out about being a big head. It was part of his training.

But Dan didn't go back to Mr. Wrinkle's after that because the story was dropped. We presumed Dan didn't need the old man's advice any more because he had learnt all the basic fundamentals. Or Mr. Wrinkle had died.

IV. Centre-Forwards

'**O**SGOOD,' they tell you behind the Fulham Road goal at Stamford Bridge, 'is good, GOOD.' A tall, lanky lad, with fuzzy, close-cropped hair, the local hero; he moves into view with an easy rolling stride gathering strength like a quarter-miler as he goes up the wing with the ball. He is more than 'good', a natural star.

Peter Osgood, a married nineteen-year old, made his dramatic appearance as No. 9 for Chelsea during the 1965-66 season and it was not long before he was gobbled up as the new golden boy, as Jimmy Greaves had been with the same club eight years before. Osgood showed he could combat this hero worship and the sweet syrup of flattery by maturing with each game rather than trying to over-do the fancy stuff in tiny bursts.

His goals, like those classic long-range efforts against A.C. Milan, in the Inter Cities Fairs Cup at Stamford Bridge; against Tottenham and Fulham and the precious header which dumb-founded the Kop in the F.A. Cup Third Round at Anfield, were taken with astonishing coolness.

Osgood is in the new school of centre-forwards and I'm not surprised that he has been referred to as another Nandor Hidegkuti. He plays deep, so deep sometimes that he is in a position to head away a dangerous shot speeding towards his own net, and when that work is done he moves away with the ball avoiding the hardest tackles as if they were minor insults unleashed by drunken bores at a cocktail party. Such fluidity of movement is expressed some-times as if his thoughts are else-where, but like the deceptive façade of many great players, it is only illusory. It is this façade which the opposition discovers to their cost when the ball is solidly in the back of their net.

Osgood's agility and smooth running matches his strength in the tackle. He does not pull out of tackles or wander around like a lost soul if momentarily pinned down by the opposition. During the F.A. Cup Fourth Round Cup-tie against Leeds in February 1966, he came loping up the wing, only, through sheer speed, to lose control of the ball so that it became a question of whether Hunter, crashing into view like a white colt, or he would reach the ball first. It was a collision to be avoided but Osgood moved on strongly and the pair jarred together with a shuddering crunch. Hunter's tackle was a brave one and the danger was averted, but Osgood's perseverance could easily have paid off.

Like all great centre-forwards, Osgood retains an almost insolent composure in the penalty area, suddenly expressing himself with a touch so cheeky that its very unexpectedness can mean death to a defensive blockade.

In a league match against West Ham which Chelsea won 6-2, Osgood made four of the goals by manufacturing elements of pure surprise. For the first goal he lazily hooked the ball over his head from out on the right flank at a moment when an ordinary player would probably have sent a plebian pass to his outside-right. Graham nonchalantly smashed the pass in.

The time will surely come before long when Osgood does all this for England, and those who canvas so fervently for his inclusion at the earliest opportunity, are not for once doing an hysterical 'Albert Quixall', the Sheffield Wednesday golden boy, blooded in the early fifties by England far, far too soon.

Osgood's technique is far from where we came in. I can still see the WM formation No. 9s after the war, having men-of-war feuds with opposing stopper-centre-halves. Tommy Lawton, the first hero, was like Osgood, a natural, who expressed his contempt for such rigid manoeuvers with methods extremely delicate and contrite for a big man, and of course there was no better header of the ball, nor has been since.

But Lawton was out of context to the general bustle of the time. Ronnie Rooke of Fulham and Arsenal was the classic opposite to Peter Osgood, a craggy, beak-faced, tousled haired, no-nonsense player in the tradition of George Camsell of Middlesbrough, who banged in over 400 goals before the War.

Ronnie, 'strong and wide' as Johnny Harris of Chelsea described him, had his best moments with the Arsenal Championship side of 1947-48, booting in Jimmy Logie's lay-ons with a ferocious leer on his face, that beaky nose stuck out with contempt, his long shirt sleeve unbuttoned flapping near his shorts, as he shot the ball into the net.

His first game for Arsenal, after being transferred from Fulham, was just before the Christmas of 1946, when Arsenal were at the foot of the table and no longer the glamour boys. The game was against Charlton at Highbury and Rooke scored the only goal, a goal from a corner battered in from his head past Sam Bartram. I can still see the picture, Rooke in the air as if suspended by a parachute in the midst, his eyes slits, his beak soaring forwards, his hair a mass of soggy black, his lips thrown wide apart like an Ava Gardner sneer.

Arsenal soon became a new team inspired by Rooke's bustle and the following season when they won the Championship he scored thirty-three goals while his own defence only conceded thirty-two goals all season.

Since the war we have had ample time to make up our minds about the type of centre-forward most pleasing to watch. There are some Anglo-Saxon bar-room chatterers who claim that the best centre-forwards are the 'wee little uns' moulded on the Hughie Gallacher legend, wee men like Charlie Wayman of Southampton and Preston, who liked the ball given to them 'on the carpet', ball players these with a vicious shot combined and ready to take to punishment from a centre-half twice their size.

Then there is an obvious preference for the lofties of the Tommy Lawton, Nat Lofthouse, John Charles school, who thrust themselves into the air and headed down into the net with a goalkeeper standing there with his mouth open and knee caps pressed together.

And another preference for smaller frames like Jackie Milburn of Newcastle, Tommy Taylor of Manchester United, Ian St John of Liverpool, Ronnie Allen of West Bromwich and Trevor Ford of Aston Villa, Sunderland and Wales, different players in their way but each wanting the ball and going after it with skill as well as strength. Trevor Ford used to batter down goalkeepers as if they were warthogs getting in the way of an elephant by a water hole, but he could use the ball with a certain grace as well. Taylor, who was killed at Munich, was a lovely player, good with his head, a delicate ball player as well, who died when his England position was seemingly secure.

'IAN ST-ER Ian ST-ER IAN SINTJERN,' they shout from the Kop as their stocky god nods home another. St John somehow contrives to head the ball when his body is horizontal to the ground, flicking the ball in off his nut as if he was nodding away a fly during an afternoon nap. His most famous point was scored in this way from Callaghan's cross to win the Cup Final for Liverpool against Leeds in 1965.

And of course mention again must be made of Bobby Smith, a tank who sent centre-halves bouncing off him with an expression of horrified innocence displayed through a toothy grin. 'Good old Bobby' won everything there was to win with Tottenham during their double heyday, a Geordie blacksmith whom I first saw play for Chelsea when he was a kid of seventeen; thinner then, more fey, but the toothy grin was already there, especially after he had bulged the net. Bobby's great art was taking the weight off the centre of the field so that an inside like Greaves could speed through the back, but he was also excellent in the air and could drive them in from all angles.

Times change and the old-time centre-forwards of the WM formations who were the lighthouses of the forward line have disappeared in preference to a deeper playing stylist directing operations, whereas before, he would have simply finished operations. A centre-forward is often part of three strikers in a 4-3-3 formation or a deep lying player in the 4-2-4 created so efficiently by Nandor Hidegkuti. Raymond Kopa did this so well for Rheims, and on a good day Don Revie of Manchester City – and now Johnny Byrne of West Ham – have performed sweetly in the back spaces.

But if the ideal all-round centre-forward has to be selected it must be Alfredo di Stefano of Real Madrid, a man of supreme energy and science was an aristocratic contempt for the hordes who tried to stop him.

He was born in Buenos Aires and played for some time with a Bogota side, Millonarios. But it was during his era with Real Madrid when men like Puskas, Gento and Raymond Kopa twinkled in a tableau around him, that this balding No. 9 reached an almost outrageous peak of perfection.

Five European Cups were won in a row inspired by those effervescent, arrogant spurts that brought di Stefano through from his own half of the field to totally destroy the opposition with a pass or shot presented in a manner always surprising.

The great naturals shoot and score at a moment least expected, when an average player would be rolling his foot back or taking deliberate aim. When Di Stefano shot he stabbed or flipped the ball, hardly moving his boot at all, gliding the ball in as if he was stamping nonchalantly on grapes. It left goalkeepers shrugging their shoulders in miserable defeat.

I can still hear his staccato commands during a match between Real Madrid and Arsenal at Highbury. They sounded like HA, HA, HA, mere barks as he rolled the ball to colleagues under the floodlight with the authority of a Spanish polo colonel at Deauville, displaying in the same way a gracious ruthlessness.

And after a Real Madrid goal so casually thumped in, Di

Stefano embracing his colleagues, arms round a neck administering a kiss with a paternal flamboyance. Another goal to the side who made the all-white strip one of the most famous of all. A goal usually made or scored by this great Argentinean himself.

V. The Hero

We used to wait for him in the car park at Stamford Bridge. Greasy schoolboys with greasy autograph books. The crowds came through the turnstiles fanning out towards the terraces and we got buffeted if we got in the way.

Near the club offices was the players' entrance and we got as close to the mouth as the on-duty official would allow. 'Go away, sonny. Move on, sonny. Come on lad.'

Half an hour before kick-off the players would drift in and we would pounce on them saying: 'Please Mr Goulden. Sign Mr Walker. Please Mr Harris.' They came in with friends, wearing long overcoats and scarves, their hair well oiled and pulled back over their ears. Tommy Walker, the pre-war Scottish international inside-right and described, not inappropriately, as 'the first gentleman of football' was the kindest. He was not a tall man and we could crane up near his face and he would smile hugely and sign all our books.

Len Goulden, the other inside forward, who had played for West Ham and England before the war, was brisk and forthcoming but signed our books as he strode towards the dressing room under the main stand talking to his friends as he walked in broad cockney, his hair parted in a thin line down the middle. John Harris was equally kind, a small smile on the edges of his mouth, a mild Scottish purr. 'Quick son. Kick-off's soon.'

They were our gods, they and the goalkeeper Harry Medhurst, the present Chelsea trainer, who bounded into the ground like a small ostrich. Harry still shows that bounding walk as he leaves the pitch after treating an injury.

The Chelsea footballers were not dandies in those days. They dressed as well as they could afford on £12-a-week maximum, which came into effect early in 1947, long overcoats with slightly spivvy shoulders, polished, solid shoes and gaudy ties.

We waited for them and for visiting players, especially if they were Stanley Matthews of Stoke, Tom Finney of Preston, or Billy Wright of Wolves, Or Stanley Mortensen of Blackpool, or Billy Steel of Derby County, men in slightly crumpled, double-breasted pin-striped suits with splashy ties that gangsters wore in Hollywood films.

But in the winter of 1946 we waited most of all for Tom Lawton, the hero of Chelsea and Stamford Bridge, and indeed, of all England.

Tom was the great professional, the goal getter, the towering athlete with the elastic head in the number nine shirt. He was unmistakable on the field, shoulders slightly hunched, his hair greased back into a solid, flattened, blob of black, his long legs dangling across the pitch, his arms flung out to take a tackle, his cheeks puffed out when he unleashed a shot. At the players' entrance we always waited for Tom.

He would come swinging through the entrance, a towering figure to those of us who had only achieved half of our ultimate height. Tall, strong, his craggy Lancashire face jutting forward slightly his long overcoat hanging down near his ankles and done up untidily with a loose, flapping belt, his hair soaking with oil so that the central parting stood out like the lane of a city highway.

Around Tom Lawton came the hangers on. I remember them in the cold weather with their neat trilbys and demob raincoats, and in the Spring with wide pinstripe suits, usually brown, and shirts with no ties with the white collars outside the jacket collars. Perhaps Tom knew them or perhaps he didn't. But they followed him devotedly in packs, one or two of them chewing matchsticks from a corner of their mouths.

Tom soared forward and we tried to stop him but he moved on gangling above us to look in on the way to the dressing rooms at the Chelsea offices. He would come out after a few minutes and the pack would move off, the hangers on lounging at his side saying: 'Good luck, Tom', 'Bang two in, Tom'. And we would go along also, but smaller and less obvious, until we lounged into the centre-forward's belly, bearing our books.

'Please Mr Lawton, Sign Mr Lawton. Oh, please Tommy.'

Mr Lawton was usually in a hurry. Although he was my hero and I dreamt of him I never found him a sympathetic character in those days when he was a football warrior of England. I never got his autograph and rarely saw him sign one for the kids. The odd one perhaps. But he didn't make a habit of it. He pushed me aside once and wouldn't sign. 'I'm in a hurry, son,' he said in broad Bolton.

Tom Lawton may have had his reasons for seeming morose. In 1946 and 1947 he was playing for Chelsea but the side was not particularly distinguished; particularly on the wings and at wing-half; Dickie Spence was in the veteran stage on the right-wing and there was virtually no left-winger to speak of, Dolding, Paton, ran themselves into the ground but they lacked class. Chelsea's saving strength lay at inside forward where Tom Lawton had Len Goulden and Tom Walker working to make him goals, and at centre-half where John Harris, the captain, was calmly efficient.

The Chelsea side under the secretary and managership of Mr William Birrell hovered round the middle of the table that season although Tom Lawton broke the club's goal-scoring record with 26 goals. What was evident was that he had incredible drawing power. The crowds, starved after five years of war, flocked to Stamford Bridge to watch the resumption of Football League soccer.

Lawton was a moody player at that time, often stating sulkily out of the game for long periods but when he did respond the effect was devastating. There would be a huge bulge in the opposition's net and Lawton would stride away with a shrug of pleasure.

The vast, open slug of a main terrace at Stamford Bridge was usually spread like a ham sandwich with humanity when Tom Lawton was on Chelsea's books. Entertainment was restricted, apart from the cinema, and soccer was one of the few attractions available. Tom Lawton playing down the Fulham Road provided one of the few pin-ups of a jaded metropolis. That soccer had lost none of its pulling power because of the war, had been proved a year before at Stamford Bridge when the Moscow Dynamos attracted over 82,000 people to the ground and many more who struggled over the barriers and stood on the roof of the main stand.

Lawton had scored an exquisite goal that day in a 3-3 draw and the London crowd had taken an instant delight in the appearance of the centre-forward who had taken over from Dixie Dean at Everton before the war and lived up to the great man's reputation as a killer inside an opponent's penalty box.

So the crowds came to watch Tommy and laugh good naturedly at Chelsea. There wasn't much else to watch. Arsenal were still looking for a team, Tottenham and Fulham were in the Second Division and Charlton, while being London's rosiest and most successful side – Cup Finalists in 1946 and Cup Winners in 1947 – were not easy to get to. So the crowds went to the Fulham Road. And Tommy wrapped up in his mountainous overcoat would stride in to please them.

It is worth looking at some of the attendances at Stamford Bridge during the autumn and winter of 1946 which ranged from 50,000 to 70,000. Lawton could not complain that he was not an attraction.

Chelsea did not get beyond the Fourth Round, losing, after a replay to Derby, when that dreadful winter had really set in. What had seemed to be a juicy opportunity for Chelsea to reach Wembley for the first time faded despite Lawton's two momentous goals against Arsenal at White Hart Lane.

Tom Lawton would leave us hanging around outside the players' dressing rooms waiting hopefully for other players to come up and perhaps sign before going in to strip. Then we would disperse and make for the terraces to squeeze in deep down near the grey-hound track behind one of the goals.

In those days Chelsea would come out with a savage rush as if some giant fist had punched them out onto the pitch. There was a flash of blue and white and the players were on the field charging as if unstoppable towards one of the goal nets. Lawton with his languid motion, found it hard to keep up with this opening rush, a tall, dominating more nonchalant figure rubbing his hands together surrounded by a number of straining colleagues. At any moment one expected the fist to come out of the tunnel and drag them all back again.

The strip of the time would have weighed down an elephant. Chelsea in heavy blue vests with white collars and sleeves down to the finger tips, sleeves which John Harris for one never rolled up, long flapping white shorts down to the kneecaps, heavy shin-guards sticking through the bulging blue stockings and on the feet the old type of heavy football boot with leather bars above the toe caps and high ankle supports.

Tom Lawton would stand there during the kick-about with his hands on his hips, occasionally volleying a practice ball languidly into the roof of the net, a look of complete unconcern on his face.

When the games were on one can remember his grace and freedom when he moved with the ball, so light across the ground for a big man. There was the game against Liverpool, who went on to win the Championship that season. Liverpool were a sturdy, if not particularly brilliant side, with the strong Scottish left-winger and Justice of the Peace Billy Liddell, Albert Stubbins, the ginger-haired opportunist at centre-forward, Balmer, a clever, bald-headed inside-forward; in defence Laurie Hughes, reliable and industrious and in goal Sidlow, the Welsh international goalkeeper.

Lawton tore Liverpool to pieces that cold January afternoon. His first goal was a typical header from such a lofty
height that a Swiss journalist exclaimed in the stand: 'We have
nobody in Switzerland who can jump like that.' The second was
off balance through a crowd of players, a typical Lawton goal,
leaning back so that the back of his head was almost touching
the turf, his shooting foot thrust at just the right angle to con-
nect with the ball and send it whirling into the corner of the
net. Chelsea won the game 3-1 and it was a match in which
Lawton showed the devastating form he had been displaying
for England that season.

There was a league match against their great rivals of
the era, Arsenal, at Stamford Bridge. The tension was to be
repeated in the Cup a few weeks later when Lawton put Chelsea
through at the third attempt. But this game was the first league
game between the clubs since the war so the crowds poured
across London and Stamford Bridge swelled uncomfortably at
the seams. Again it was Lawton who won the day for Chelsea
and his second goal was a mad piece of opportunism.

Dunkley, in a *Daily Mirror* cartoon of the time, sketched
the afternoon's events. 'Nearly 60,000 demob macks paraded at
Stamford Bridge on Saturday but were dismissed before being
thoroughly tested. In fact the sun broke through just before the
game started and Chelsea broke through just after, Bernard Joy
slipped up – Spence slipped through and Lawton slipped it in.

'The sun then disappeared and Chelsea started missing
things but at a (Arsenal) corner kick were so determined to
mislay Compton they forgot all about Lewis. Near full time as
most of the "3 draws" pool boys were wondering if their other
two have clicked – Lawton upset their coupons by playing a
"Joe Davis" two angled shot into the pocket. I am not suggesting that Arsenal should take up billiards – their fans are already
after me – so you tell 'em!

Arsenal were still a struggling side that day, but within a
year, with the addition of players like Joe Mercer, and craggy

Ronnie Rooke and Dan Roper they would be advancing firmly towards their sixth Championship.

The Bolton boy continued to entertain the Stamford Bridge crowds as the pitches grew to ice in the miserable early spring of 1947 and onto the extended season which grew into May. There was another memorable game on a pitch of powdery snow when Wolverhampton Wanderers came to the Bridge with Stanley Cullis on his last playing season at centre-half, Billy Wright boyish at right-half, and Hancocks and Mullen on the wings.

Wolverhampton looked a superb combination in their old global strip on the pitch which gleamed like white wedding cake. Lawton went round Cullis once and drove an unstoppable shot past Bert William but generally Wolverhampton had the ascendancy. The menace of Hancocks and Mullen on the wings, which Cullis was to exploit so forcefully later, predominated. The speed of these two wingers was devastating and Chelsea, who fielded Willy Steffen, the Swiss international left-back, who played a number of games for them that winter, found it hard to counteract these rapier thrusts.

Stanley Cullis's baldhead disappeared into the Stamford Bridge tunnel for the last time. It was not long before the Chelsea crowd was to see the last of Tom Lawton as a resident player.

The blow was struck during the summer of 1947, after the Great Britain-Rest of Europe match at Hampden Park, where Lawton with two goals had helped to shatter what little Continental opposition there was so soon after the war. The England team subsequently had another devastating win by 10-0 against Portugal in Lisbon, where our hero banged in four goals and the Portuguese players were so upset afterwards that they refused to attend the official banquet.

Suddenly the headlines were that Lawton wanted to leave Chelsea. We, who waited outside the Chelsea gates during an August heat-wave, waiting for the Chelsea players to report for training, were shattered. We stared gloomily towards the club offices as old newspapers floated by in the hot breeze down the Fulham Road.

But the fact remained that Lawton had asked for a transfer which Chelsea eventually admitted in a club programme at the start of the season. 'Tommy Lawton's name is very much in printer's ink this week. Statement and counter-statements have been issued, and what should remain a domestic matter between the parties concerned has become overnight a question of public auction. Known facts are these: Lawton has, since the invited press statement, expressed definitely that he desires a change. The Board in due coarse will consider that desire and reach a decision.'

We who regarded Lawton as something of a god could not understand this act of disloyalty. We regarded his auction with the one-sided incomprehension of a lover who has been jilted.

Lawton was bid for and bid for by Blackburn, Sunderland and Arsenal, and the papers were full of rumours, but eventually it was Notts County, the Third Division club who paid £20,000 for our centre-forward. Lawton, a shrewd businessman, did well out of this deal as his skill deserved, with a house and an outside job, and Notts County did themselves a good turn also because they gained promotion before he left them.

But we who were not adults could never understand our hero going. It took us, like some emotional breakups, about a year to get over it. The car park wasn't the same any more,. The tall figure wasn't there any more with his long overcoat and almost in-approachable mysticism. And neither were the hangers on.

When he came back to London, first to Brentford, then to Arsenal, we had grown up and he wasn't the same attraction and besides he was an *old* man growing into his thirties, and he wasn't in the England side any more. There were new discoveries by then, wing-half Ken Armstrong, who had kept Lawton for a while out of the Chelsea attack shortly before his transfer, with the displays of opportunism, and then there was Roy Bentley, the lithe, blonde, shy young inside-forward who came to Stamford Bridge from Newcastle as an inside-forward.

Chelsea came to depend on Roy Bentley and he eventually did a great deal to win them the Football League Championship in 1955. Bentley used to sign our autograph book staring coyly down at the paper as he signed. It was always the same after he scored a goal for Chelsea. He hung his head like a naughty boy.

Bentley became a wandering centre in the Chelsea forward line, and for a while he was very effective. He would cut out towards the wings and a big man like Hugh Billington would be waiting up in the goalmouth to convert his centres. In later years Bentley became more direct leaving his wingers Parsons and Blunstone to use the flanks.

Looking back, Lawton still remains the original hero. He was one of the great centre-forwards, perfectly equipped, light on his feet, his elastic neck able to direct the ball to a waiting colleague or into just the spot where a goalkeeper could not reach it, an opportunist who could turn a game with a goal shot from a ludicrous angle. He learnt much playing inside-right to Dixie Dean when he went to Everton in the thirties.

The hero was six-foot tall and weighed just over 12 stones in his prime. He cost Chelsea £11,500 when they signed him from Everton on 7 November 1945. He came to take over the tradition of great centre-forwards at Chelsea, following George Hilsdon, George Mills, Hughie Gallacher and Joe Payne.

Lawton was a completely different build to Gallacher, who was small, bouncy, aggressive, a wonderful ball player. But unlike him, Lawton usually kept his temper on the field.

Lawton, like Gallacher, did not find Chelsea a congenial club to settle with. There were rumours of dressing room tension at the time of the transfer. Lawton had a reputation for speaking his mind.

So big Tom went and we mourned.

And I never got his autograph.

VI. White Hart Lane

That Spring night was moist and dirty; the street lamps of Tottenham flinging jaundiced streaks of yellow against rows and rows of battered, toy-box Victorian houses. It was one of the first nights of Spring, after the savage cold spell of 1963, and the night of the European Cup Winners Cup quarter-final, second leg, between Tottenham Hotspur and Slovan Bratislava of Czechoslovakia at White Hart Lane.

Tottenham had something to fight for, having lost the first leg 2–0, but there was strong reason to suppose that they could pull back the deficit in front of their own crowd, and that was the intriguing reason I and a friend were stuck in a traffic jam not far out of Manor House on the path to Tottenham, with thousands of other souls.

We were caught in a human avalanche bowling down Tottenham High Road, in cars, taxis and motor scooters, and when the distance became appropriate, men on foot shuffling forward, talking to each other, or themselves.

My friend at the wheel had a chubby face into which his lips sometimes disappeared, especially when he was in a good mood. The face would lose its lips and then you knew he was smiling. Sometimes the lips disappeared when he was angry as well. Stuck in that traffic jam I could sense he was becoming more and more irritable because he had no lips, only a cheroot sticking out of a tiny hole between two bounding cheeks.

Inching forward against mudguards of other rivals, lash-ing the wheel so that the car could turn at sudden desperate angles, cursing and belting – 'you shit', at other drivers hunched in their overcoats beyond only thinly diaphanous windscreens, my friend got me to White Hart Lane or rather one of those winding terraces near the ground where the houses give way to cars on match days. There were five minutes to go until kick-off, but we still had a fair walk.

We got out of the car and crossed a main road where late-comers were scurrying in hysterical clumps and we became part of them, assuming their identity, hunching our shoulders, sticking out our chins and uttering vague platitudes about the coming game below our breath.

Skirting a small untidy, twisted park, we could see the flood-light pylons raging now with silver light above the trees. There was a sudden gush of uplifted sound flowing into a monumen-tal roar which swept across the skyline, hanging there for one ecstatic second, then falling to a low, orgasmic moan.

'That wasn't a goal,' said my friend wheezing slightly, be-cause we were now trotting along like two cab horses. 'The roar wasn't long enough. It hangs there for five minutes after a goal.'

There was another roar but more muted, it dawdled, rose clucking and then descended to a thin whir like the embers of a softly burning squib. 'Tottenham ought to get those goals,' my friend said as we broke put of the brick and came out into Tottenham High Road. 'The crowd will beat Slovan. Jesus, listen to that.'

The noise had become mountainous, swollen, almost obscene; draining the blood of that night from every living North London thing outside the stadium so that they became uncommitted ghosts.

Quick, quick, slow, quick, quick, slow – down Tottenham High Road we sped below the sound where there remained only the souvenirs of a giant, passing human wave; peanuts, cartons, newspaper, severed hot dogs and odd clumps of people hanging round trying to buy tickets from expressionless, unsympathetic touts.

We had our tickets, good ones in the East stand and we made off towards the open gash of the stadium entrance as the roar became a continuous crashing symphony, booming up and over the stands and bouncing down into the streets below. 'Have they scored?' I bellowed to an old man with a peaked cap crouching on the East-stand steps.

'No, but Bobby Smith's done the 'keeper.'

We jerked and heaved through the turnstiles and raced upstairs until we came to the gap, where the scene suddenly hit the eye in a panorama of raging colour. As the steward took our tickets and said: 'Over there, sir, in that block,' we saw the pitch burnt out by the cold winter and now a streak of brown; on it men and white of Tottenham Hotspur streaking through the Slovan defence.

Across the pitch thousands of faces congealed into one lump of plasticine, emitted a fearful screech.

'Come on mate, sit down,' said several voices, and we gasped and grunted down below until our bottoms squeezed onto wood. Below was the game on the park, the game played by professionals of genius with beautifully, poised control, a game of fascination unfolding in which Tottenham were gambling on a tactical plan to continue in this competition.

Marchi, captaining the side in place of the injured Blanch-flower at right-half, was not out of place governing the orchestra with sound authority, while Mackay on the other flank burst forward again and again, his barrel chest stuck out, his legs streak-ing across the turf like the hooves of a hunter.

We watched anxiously as the Czechs mounted a series of retaliatory attacks with the powerful Molnar mashing his way through, on odd, destructive forays. It seemed certain that if the Czechs got another goal it would dampen the night. They were massive athletes inspired by their giant centre-half Popluhar and were in no mood to bow to the roar of the crowd.

As the minutes advanced towards half time, their World Cup goalkeeper, Wilhelm Schroiff, although clearly unsettled by the early charges of the massive, buccaneering Bobby Smith, had not yet yielded a goal.

Tottenham at this stage played a quick-passing game, Greaves, Smith and Jones wasted no time in firing shots with the rapidity of tennis professionals making powerful smashes. *Oh* and *Oh* and *Oh* spewed from the crowd but no goal came and the castle walls of Slovan remained unbroken.

But ten minutes before the half came the first moment of grandeur; the first moment of break-through for which the Tottenham side had worked so passionately. It was scored typically by Mackay, who got hold of a misdirected clearance by Popluhar outside the penalty area and scored with a mighty shot. Around us men in natty blue coats rose in unison squeezing their thumbs into the soft, yielding flesh of each other's craniums, waving cigars, losing cigars, choking with ecstasy, oh, Dave, oh Dave, good old Dave. And Mackay leaping in the air, was hugged by everyone of the Tottenham side except Bill Brown in goal, who gave his own little wave of pleasure from far away on the other side of the playing valley. And the game was on again with Tottenham in with a chance, that first brick out of the castle wall.

The crowd at White Hart Lane, that ground of the two high main stands, which seem to impose their authority over the pitch like the bridges of Queensborough and Brooklyn over the East River of New York, summoned up all their energy, screamed for more goals, and Tottenham fought on. Time hardly advanced before Jimmy Greaves scored one of his own exquisite, individual efforts, collecting a pass in midfield and beating two defenders on his run before squeezing the ball past Schroiff. And then came another goal as the stands shook, a goal that seemed likely all along headed in by Bobby Smith, who got his bulk up above the despairing reach of Schroiff to head into the net, so that Schroiff almost broke apart, despair and agony on his face, and Smith ran back to the centre, a huge toothy grin on his face, his colleagues running their hands through his curly, greasy hair. In that ten-minute burst, Slovan had been shattered and the crowd now were singing Glory, Glory, HALLelujah, THE SPURS GO MARCHING ON.

And now on into the second half, with Tottenham vastly on top, dictating their terms with quick-passing movements which spilt over the drying retaliation of those large, competent defenders, Popluhar, Urban and Jankovic. And inspiring to the Tottenham assaults was White, 'the ghost' as they called him, who was killed tragically by lightning on a golf course in 1964, a player of astonishing fluidity who appeared from nowhere, from gaps of sheer impossibility to crack open a defensive wall.

White had the game in the palm of his hand working on it like a sculptor in possession of a clarified lump of form. Alongside him, Saul, Smith, Greaves and Jones showered hostility on the Slovan defense, and at the other end the threat of Molnar, a robust, busy centre-forward had been squashed by the gargantuan Norman. It was over surely, one more and Tottenham were assured of a semi-final place.

And the goal came, scored with devastating nonchalance by greaves. Schroiff, poor Schroiff, had rushed out to retrieve a ball he punched away from Smith, but as he bounded forward, Greaves got possession on the edge of the penalty area and fired the ball over the goalkeeper's bald head and into the net.

The courageous, agile Schroiff fell back on to the ground, his pride shattered as grocers from Willesden bayed and hooted from the stands. His heart had been ripped out, despair hovered over his face, one hand scratched at his brow, he looked so forlorn that spectators of the neutral breed mourned for him, but there were few neutrals there. There was only mild sympathy from the crowd, who would have hated him had he stopped everything.

The night was now adjusted, more composed although the Tottenham chant was as unrelenting as Muzak but never, never soft. There were two more goals from Jones and, as a reward for his momentous evening, White. The game descended into the formality of Tottenham brushing their way into the Slovan penalty area and having a bang. Then the whistle Tottenham 6, Slovan 0.

The crowd bounced onto the pitch waving and hugging the Tottenham heroes, there was perhaps a sense of anticlimax, the moments of motion were now being replaced by avid post-mortems by less authoritative lips. The boots had done their work, now it was the turn for the lips.

Schroiff left the field, for a moment, a broken man consoled on the way towards the tunnel by Bobby Smith, who had made him lose his nerve from that first moment when he had bounced into him under a shower of light. The players disappeared from view and we started pushing and shoving to go home, the gangways sucking us up reluctantly like an old man with indigestion eating an orange.

It was a night when my friend and I decided to celebrate with oysters in Soho because it was a night of absolute dominance by an English side, a night of rejuvenation after so many years of humiliation when the speedy passing of the Tottenham side had broken down the authoritative Slovan defence.

The great mass moving away from White Hart Lane, through an anonymous, drab, bingo world of London, in taxis, trains and buses had been given an excessive treat which their wives would find on their faces as they walked flushed, and garrulous out of the spring night, beer on their breath.

And eventually breaking away from this animated, receding tide, we reached Soho where we found the oysters of Wheelers soft and luscious and each one of the dozen a tiny reminder of Bill Nicholson (manager): Brown (goal): Hopkins, Henry, Marchi, Norman, Mackay, Saul, White, Smith, Greaves and Jones.

My friend's lips disappeared again as he popped another oyster into his mouth, a few, tiny chips from the sea bed sticking to his chin. After consuming one oyster and leaning back so that I saw his Adam's apple jerk forward and then recede, he murmured: 'I always thought the Newcastle side of 1951-52 was the best, but not after tonight. This Spurs team is the best British club side since the war.'

My friend was a racing man and rarely went to football matches, but as a young journalist in Newcastle he had covered some of those games when Newcastle captained by Joe Harvey burst upon the scene with their all-out attacking sallies with 'wor' Jack Milburn booting in the goals either set up by himself or set up for him.

More bits of salty liquid fell away from my friend's lips and for once the horses were forgotten. 'I came down to White Hart Lane in 1952 when Newcastle knocked Spurs out of the Cup. You couldn't get better performances than that, but tonight I changed my mind. This was even better than that one. I went back to Newcastle on the train after that game and they were being sick in the corridors and sighing, "Wor Jackie Milburn, wor Jackie", and "Wor Frank Brennan, wor Frank". We had beaten the push and run boys with our long ball and felt great. But tonight was superb, the finest. Newcastle wouldn't have won that game in 1952, with Mackay, White and Greaves playing as they did tonight.'

'A delightful result,' said the restaurant manager looking at us across the bar. 'They ought to win that Cup now, don't you think. My money's on them.'

They did, of course, beating Atletico Madrid 5-1 in Rotterdam, with Danny Blanchflower back as captain. But having seen the game against Slovan, we knew it all along.

VII. The Matthews Final

'The greatest of all time', *meraviglioso* Matthews–
Stoke City, Blackpool and England.
Expressionless enchanter, weaving as on strings
Conceptual patterns to a private music, heard
Only by him, to whose slowly emerging theme
He rehearses steps, soloist in compulsions of a dream.
ALAN ROSS

Michael, a writer, who has long since established and distinguised himself in the field of criticism, gave a tea party in St John's Wood in May 1953, for the Cup Final between Bolton and Blackpool. In those days television sets were rare and to watch meant laboring half across London – the father-in-law of a distant relation.

On this occasion the writer, who had not shaved for several days and who perpetually wore an old American combat jacket and trousers bought off the peg at Woolworths, persuaded his father, a reserved, successful Jewish antique dealer, to give a tea party for a few friends so we could watch the match.

The interest before the match was enormous, because Stanley Matthews was having yet another attempt at winning a Cup Final and seemed certain to do so at this time because Bolton appeared far below the class of Manchester United and Newcastle who had beaten Blackpool at Wembley in '48 and '51.

The father agreed, and on that lovely sunny afternoon, a

number of taxis converged on Swiss Cottage, branching off
from the main traffic towards Wembley, to rest outside a high
block of flats with a view over London.

We went up in the lift and pressed the bell; the door slithered against carpet and a small man stood there wearing an
immaculate waistcoat and superbly cut suit. He smiled like
Picasso, his baldhead soft and shining, his affability as we
entered spreading itself round the luxury of the flat carefully
decorated with china, antiques and prints. Out of the window,
across an expanse of rooftops splashed grey in the sunshine,
was Lords cricket ground.

'Michael's not arrived yet,' said Mr. H. And we were not
surprised because Michael was never early. Two men sat round
Mr. H.'s hearth very different in shape and size but by now
wearing casual clothes, grey flannel trousers with bits of paint
on them, excessive ties, their fingers brown with nicotine; they
were Robert, a landscape painter and Louis, a writer.

We all knew each other well and needed no introduction
from Mr. H., being habitués of the Gorgon and the Colony
Room in Soho, and the Queen's Elm in Chelsea. In fact, two
of us had been in the Gorgon Club the night before, and we
looked like it.

Mr. H. tacked from the room and reappeared with a sherry
decanter. He was in no way disturbed by the voraciousness of
his guests. He might have been surprised at the rate at which
the sherry disappeared but his smile never left his face.

When Mr. H. again left the room Robert said: 'I wish
Henrietta would stop throwing plates. It's the second time she's
cut me.' He lowered his head and there at the base of the skull
was a dirty piece of Elastoplast over which thick, unruly hair
wove together into a thicket.

'She's getting very violent. She must be in love with you.'

'Hum,' said Robert.

'It's incredible what they put up with at the Gorgon,' said
Louis. 'Old N. came in the other night dressed as a parson and

danced with Bill and he wasn't turned out.'

Mr. H. reappeared and he might have heard and he might not, but he was determined to make us feel at home. Mrs. H., a heavy, warm woman, wearing a flowery tea dress, slipped into the room moving like a wary ostrich. We rose with some difficulty, due to our physical condition and Mrs. H. shook hands with us running her eyes over each new guest with quiet horror. 'Michaels' friends, she must have been thinking, 'Michael's friends.'

Mr. H. turned the television set on with some gusto twenty minutes before kick off, and Wembley came into view with the top of the stadium shown against the brown fluorescence of the set, flags waving, the crowd singing 'Abide with me'. We stared politely.

'Perry and Mortensen will decide it.'

None of us thought Bolton would win. They were too solid and obvious and all depended upon Lofthouse. 'The Lion of Vienna', after that wonderful winning goal he scored for England against Austria the year before. Lofthouse was always tremendously dangerous, but Blackpool had the obvious talent. I had seen them beat Arsenal in the sixth round; they had played superbly that day, winning by Alan Brown's goal which he scored falling over Kelsey and breaking his leg.

Brown was watching this game from the touchline. The teams were given in the paper I had brought along as a programme.

Michael arrived with ten minutes to go, as Prince Philip was being presented to the teams. The roar that greeted them resounded out of every crack of Mr. H.'s set. Rushing into the room he immediately took over the situation, chin surprisingly shaved. His combat jacket bulging with cigarette packets of newspaper.

Mrs. H. slipped gratefully from the room while Mr. H. hovered in the rear and Michael immediately suggested an elaborate betting system for the game. We all drew a player and the player to score first would win the jackpot. This was to be carried on after each goal.

I drew Mortensen and felt safe because if anybody scored first Morty would. Michael drew Moir of Bolton, and said 'Bugger'. The drawing of bets was carried on with great urgency. We were introduce by Mr. H. to a girl relative and her boyfriend; when she sat down I noticed her legs were firm and she crossed them well without shyness, but her young man sat down with some difficulty as if his underpants were too tight for him.

The teams were lining up and there was a buzz from the stadium, the sound of a practice ball being kicked off the field, Matthews there out on the other side of the stadium rubbing his hands and toeing the ground. 'Poussin's landscapes are extraordinarily naïve. Coubert's a different proposition,' said Michael slumping down beside Robert. 'Leave painting till afterwards,' I childishly yelped.

'John, you're not conductive to conversation,' said Michael. The referee blew his whistle.

A Cup Final had begun.

Mr. H. watched with that smile still fixed on his face, his small body perfectly set in his chair. Miss H. looked on with somewhat bored detachment while the boy friend licked his lips. Our group all leaned forward making little comments, 'Come on Stan,' I said. The ball made a tump thumping sound in the television like firm punching in a boxing ring. Michael got out a dirty handkerchief and wiped his ample forehead because he was inclined to sweat profusely. 'Bolton will win because they'll frighten Black-pool. Blackpool are too neurotic. Matthews never plays at Wembley. I wonder about Poussin, I wonder? As for your Humphrey Lyttelton young Moynihan, why don't you discover Charlie Parker?

Bolton scored immediately. Michael was scratching his stomach, Robert lighting another cigarette, Louis staring out of the window and Mr H. rising for some reason or another.

Lofthouse caught Farm off balance with a gentle shot and the ball spun away from the goalkeeper's fingers into the net.

It was reticent Louis' money, and he got up and squealed: 'GULL, GULL, give me the money.' Michael looked flushed: 'Bugger,' he said as Lofthouse disappeared into a mob of congratulatory players.

'What a silly goal,' said Miss H.

'They left the fucking man unmarked,' said Michael. 'What can you expect. I told you Blackpool were neurotic.'

'I dare say Bolton will win easily now,' said Robert teasing Michael. Michael bet Robert a pound they wouldn't. He made another hasty draw for the next goal but when it came, Blackpool's equalizer, we weren't quite sure at first who to give the money to. It certainly seemed that Mortensen had driven the ball in but the ball was diverted on the way by a Bolton defender. At any rate Robert had Mortensen and we gave him the money. Before half time Moir nudged in another goal for Bolton, so Blackpool went in finding the clock surprisingly against them.

At half time Mrs. H. brought in an astonishing tea set, all pink and white china, with a tea cosy the size of her bottom and there was much rattling and polite talk and Mr. H. got up to help her.

Michael sat still, his eyes darting from person to person. Occasionally he sucked his thumb or chewed a non-existent nail and always his eyes were boring in with some fresh question, silent or put into voluminous words. He was a heavy man for his age, which was below thirty, and was worried about it.

'You're getting far too fat, Michael,' said Robert. 'I'm getting a £40 suit made to hide it,' said Michael sadly. 'I'm afraid I'll have to sell a painting.'

The bands were playing on the pitch and we had not found much to enthuse about. Bolton had done well but Blackpool were far below form, stodgy and nervous; Matthews had only been loitering, never fierce. I went out to the toilet and on the way Mr. H. beckoned me into the dining room. He led me over to the cabinet and pointed to a round hole in the bottom corner. 'A bomb splinter did that during the Blitz,' he said, running a finger round the edge of the hole and beaming up at me at the same time. 'I've kept it as a souvenir of war.'

Mr. H. pondered over the hole lost for a moment in his own dreams, and I said something polite to bring him back to earth. In the next room there was a roar" 'Oh bugger.' Mr. H. shuddered perceptibly and I reversed out of the room where Michael was standing visibly berserk. Mrs. H. was nowhere to be seen but the girl was carefully nibbling a piece of cake like a large, engaging koala bear. On the television screen the bands were disintegrating into retreating blobs as the teams lined up again.

Michael sat down, his eyes burning into the screen and we joined in the tension and became part of it. Mr. H. too had disappeared. Eric Bell, the Bolton left half was injured, and Bolton had re-organized their side. They still had enough energy in them to give a third goal, and the scorer incredibly was Bell, limping but effective enough to push the ball into the net. Michael looked distraught, Robert inflamed with the thought of his bet made breezy remarks. 'Bolton are an insufferable side,' said Michael, 'but effective, brave.'

The ball was kicked off again and the game became a matter of grave concern for Blackpool who had made the simple things look difficult with men who would normally have enough combined combustion and skill to overpower a team as straight and narrow as Bolton. The minutes went by and we sat on the sofa and in the chairs roaring them on, even Robert. 'Oh, get in there,' 'Come on Stan.' 'Oh for Christ's sake,' as Mortensen missed a chance.

'I can't stand this,' said Michael getting to his feet. I can't, I can't.' Mr. and Mrs. H. were still out of the room. Their living room was now like a smoky gambling den in Soho, with half-filled tea cups, cake crumbs, cigarette ends and musty breath

hanging over the scene. The television set, despite the monotonous commentary, was on fire.

'Taylor to Mudie, now on to Matthews…' Blackpool were
driving themselves forward with Harry Johnston, the captain,
encouraging from the rear, a bloody company commander
yelling for a last assault. Bolton were on their knees but the
score was now 3-1.

'It's no good,' said Michael. 'I don't think they'll do it,' said
Miss H. 'Poor Matthews,' said Louis through his teeth. Thirteen
minutes from the end, with Bells' limp having transformed him
into a tragic kangaroo, Blackpool got the second goal through
Mortensen, a shot squeezed in with the utmost difficulty. But
we rose in unison and the household of Mr. and Mrs. H. was
shaken by a peculiar bellow of pleasure.

The match went on and our palms began to sweat. 'They'll
make it extra time now,' said Michael. 'Not a hope,' said Robert.
'Oh come on, please, come,' said Miss H.

I felt the tension building as Matthews started to play and
play and weave and move past man after man and the pitch
even on that small set seemed to push Matthews towards us
and out into the room so that tiny, weaving figure was now the
prince of the earth. He had literally taken over the world at that
moment our world, everybody's world.

Three minutes from the end of normal time the walls of
Mr. H.'s living room swayed, china shook, cakes fell on the floor
and men with expansive waists were seen holding each other
round the waits and dancing and screaming: 'GULL, GULL, it's
in, you swines, bitch, it's in, oh luverly.'

'What happened,' said Mr. H. looking meekly into the room.

'Mortensen's equalized,' I roared. 'What a shot.'

It indeed had been a shot, driven in from outside the
box into the top of Hanson's net so that the net swerved as
if caught by a sudden typhoon. Mortensen disappeared into
an emotional human patch of pleasure on the screen and it
was something like ours. Michael however had changed pace.

'I can't understand it,' he said. 'Why didn't Bolton line up. An absurd goal. I would never have allowed my side to let in a goal like that. Arsenal would never have done, Copping, Male, or Hapgood would have charged it down.'

It was then that Matthews set off on his run which remains one of those classics of the game, a move in which the game which had now become almost his became irrevocably his. Bolton were scattered around the field like becalmed yachts and Barrass, at one stage, had fallen to his knees feigning injury and occasionally looking up to see if the referee was watching. The television detected this in all its poignancy. But Matthews was away cutting past the exhausted Barrass and his centre swept along the ground to Perry and the ball was in the net.

This time Mr. H.'s. living room lost its final composure as men seized cushions and hugged them to their bellies, and Miss H. gave a tinkling laugh of pleasure. Somebody farted and Mr. H. looked round the door and said" 'What's happened?'

'They've won, Blackpool have done it, done it. Good old Stan. Oh lovely Stan.' The room was electric, the television screen swarming with Blackpool players hugging and embracing and we were hugging and embracing and Miss H's young man was on his feet, his neck darting backwards and forwards like a heron's beak in flight.

'Oh how exciting,' said Miss H.

'Sensational,' said Mr. H. beaming. Michael was sprawled on the sofa wiping his forehead and giggling gently to himself with Robert's quid lying on his fly-buttons. Robert was shaking hands with Louis and I was staring at the screen talking to myself and the screen was still full of waving figures and hats going in the air and mutters below the television cameras of joy like hippos having a bath and the noise was all over London and in Blackpool and Stoke and all over the country and Matthews was king and there was hardly time to start the game again before it was all over and Harry Johnston was holding the cup aloft and they were carrying Stan across the stadium. We all flopped back exhausted.

Mrs. H. came back into the room having missed the match and saw sweat and men's chests heaving and eyes glazed and her living room looking like a pigsty and she sniffed and looked alarmed and asked what had happened and we told her about Matthews but she didn't register.

'I'm glad you enjoyed the football match,' she said. 'Would anyone like some more tea?'

VIII. Centre-Half

> Ocwirk had no real position
> But his name went through Europe
> Like a prairie fire
> Leaving the charred grass of his fame
> The burnt out stubble of his roving feats.
> BRIAN HIGGINS

Centre-half to me means Leslie Compton, the former England and Arsenal rocky mountain. Les was wicket-keeper for Middlesex for many years, but he was a better foot-baller and one of the chief concerns in Arsenal's Football League Championship victory in 1947-48, and the F.A. Cup win against Liverpool in 1950.

Les was a regular full-back until 1945 when he was convert-ed to centre-half for Arsenal's match against B.A.O.R. in 1945, a bit of perception by Tom Whittaker, who felt that there was a player ideally suited to playing at mountains.

When Bernard Joy, a shrewd, blond former England-Amateur centre-half stood down from the Arsenal side short-ly after the Football League programme had started up, to become a perceptive soccer journalist, Compton took over the No. 5 shirt regularly, and in 1950 was capped for England at the tender age of 38.

I used to hate Les as a boy. Based behind the net, we saw him heading the ball away from Tommy Lawton and Roy Bent-ley as the ball came over from the corner with a contemptuous boomph from his square-shaped head. His hair was curly and soaked, surely with the hair-oil his brother Denis advertised with some flamboyance in the advertising hoardings.

Many a side fumed and battered away at the mountain that was Les, but he often stood twelve feet high and they couldn't get past him even if three of them had a go at the same time. And if Les was beaten by a crafty player like Charlie Wayman of Preston or Jackie Milburn of Newcastle, the Arsenal defence surrounding Les, Laurie Scott, Wally Barnes, Alex Forbes and sometimes Les Smith, would wheel round and cover the danger in one blanket movement of destruction.

It was the era of the third-back game in which the stopper centre-half was a pivot, a solid immobile figure. The England centre-half of the time, Neil Franklin of Stoke, was a more subtle player, often alarming the conventional backroom of bosses of his own club, by actually coming up and joining an attack occasionally. No, it didn't do then.

The good old stopper in a WM formation was supposed to stay put with eyes feasting on the rival centre-forward like a casino manager watching a con man. I can still hear the tackles meted out on No. 9's by Jack Chisholm of Brentford, Allenby Chilton (Manchester United) and Frank Brennan (Newcastle). Good, strong, solid tackling, biff, bang, crunch to make a centre-forward know he was in a game.

Another stopper was John Harris of Chelsea, with his sleeves rolled impeccably down to the end of his fingers, one of the reasons why Chelsea were not relegated immediately after the war. He believed in tidy, orderly play in which he stuck to a centre-forward like a leech, but rarely went in unfairly. His black hair smoothed back, he was often left to cope with some appalling Chelsea defensive mistakes. But the only time I saw him lose his temper was at Molineux in 1950, when a shot by Johnny Hancocks managed to beat the sleepy Chelsea defensive wall. He stood there yelling his head off.

One of Johnny's days was at Stamford Bridge, in the same

year, when the fiery Trevor Ford had been bought by Sunderland from Aston Villa for a huge fee. Chelsea had been after Ford for them-selves but failed to meet Sunderland's bid.

Ford's first game ironically was at Stamford Bridge, and Johnny Harris quietly put Ford out of the game. It was a polished, unemotional performance and totally effective. Ford was reduced to chasing loose balls.

Soon after the war Johnny, who is now the manager of Sheffield United, wrote a passage in *Improve Your Football* which goes to show how styles changed today: 'I insist, from conviction, that the centre-half in the modern game is first and foremost a stopper of the opposing centre-forward. While it might be said that this is the real starting point of his game, however, it is by no means the finishing point.

'Just when it is necessary for the centre-half to leave the opposing centre-forward to look after himself—or rather, to be looked after by some other member of the team—must be decided by circumstances. If an opposing winger has broken clear of his immediate opponents, threatening danger, the centre-half may have to decide to go out to him, but he only comes to that decision if he has a good chance of getting the ball. Otherwise, it is generally better tactics to retreat towards goal...'

A centre-half in modern football is not governed by such rigid rules of behaviourism. Now that football is more flexible and defenders in 4-2-4 or 4-3-3 formations are constantly switching and providing two or three times as much cover, a centre-half need not feel that he is running a risk in neglecting a beauty spot just beyond his own penalty area by moving laterally towards the wings or sprinting up through the middle.

The present centre-half of Leeds and England, Jackie Charlton, plays a spherical game on a line lapping both penalty spots and the flags on the half-way line. He roars round this circle like a speedway rider, in turn mopping up rival attacks and coming up the other end, often via the wings, to attack the opposing goal or take a thrusting header.

A centre-half on the attack was quite a novelty when I first started watching football and we used to stand up and exclaim with horror if we saw our beloved stopper cross the river into enemy territory. Once when Harris got his gleaming head to a corner at Stamford Bridge to put Chelsea level against Blackpool the crowd squealed with pleasure and astonishment – and then yelled at Harris to get back.

As he wrote in his book: 'When Chelsea are favourably placed I don't go up into the opposing goalmouth when my club has been awarded a corner kick. Such a coarse would be running an un-necessary risk of leaving a vital part of my centre-half job un-attended. But I do go up to add weight and possible confusion to the opposition if the side is desperately in need of a goal. Tactics should be dictated by circumstances.'

At the end of the forties Ernst Ocwirk of Austria was revealed to us as a centre-half who didn't play centre-half. Those explorers who had seen him said he played centre-forward with No. 5 on his back and that only went to confuse us who were always in the belief that the only centre-halves worth having were men who stood upright, stiff and unobliging in front of their own custodians.

But Ocwirk, whose international career for Austria stretched from 1945 to 1956, soon to put us right, was the chief spokesman in the Austrian (or Ocwirk) framework exposed at Wembley in 1951, when England were held to a 2-2 draw.

Ocwirk, 'tall, dark and determined' as John Arlott described him, a flamboyant attacking athlete played out a constructive ubiquitous role in front of Happel, who wore the No. 3 shirt as a conventional stopper centre-half game in covering Lofthouse. Ocwirk became a legend in the game and seeing him play had the same sort of meaning as F. Scott Fitzgerald's pleasure in *Meeting Cole Porter in the Ritz*.

England was slow to understand that a centre-half could be anything but static, and their selection of Leslie Compton for the England side against Yugoslavia in 1950, at Highbury, was like delivering an ageing antelope to a gang of cheetahs.

Poor Harry Johnston of Blackpool, a loyal, polished player, converted with success to the No. 5 role from wing-half, felt the real icy winds against Hungary in 1953 at Wembley, when Nandor Hidegkuti, playing as a deep lying No. 9 in the 4-2-4 system, left him to shiver in misery.

Since those times the *l'arriere* central post in international foot-ball has been manned by some original masters combing skilled defence and originality in attack. After Parola of Italy and Ocwirk, of course, came Luis Bellini, who captained Brazil in the 1958 World Cup, Jose Santamaria of Real Madrid, Jan Popluhar of Czechoslovakia, and the gaucho figure of Benfica and Portugal with moustache and sideboards, Germano.

In desperation England drafted Billy Wright from wing-half to centre-half and the move was a roaring success. The blonde, diminutive, carpet-making boy legend from Wolverhampton, nestled into the position as though he had been living there all his life. I remember one of his last games for Wolverhampton when he was marking Tom Finney who was playing himself near retirement in the No. 9 role. Tom ran like a dodgem car, but Billy was always there, squashing without a trace of generosity, each idea delivered up by his rival.

And another match when he was marking John Charles (the gentle giant) in the 1954 international against Wales at Wembley, he had the task of marking a player enjoying one of his most splendid days. Charles, who later switched to centre-half when Daniel was injured, scored two goals in that match, a hostile, massive, ball-playing giant, who bashed his way through the England defence again and again, but Wright clung to the task and one tackle when Charles had seemingly sped past him, a late slide tackle which took the ball cleanly off the Welshman's toes like a gust of wind flicking a piece of straw off a barn roof, stands out as the tackle of twenty years watching. England won 4-2 despite Charles that day, and they did so because of Wright.

IX. What it means...

It was a nasty brutal October Sunday. Dramatic black clouds plodded in oily battalions over Chelsea as heavy rain turned streets into mirrors and pedestrians into sea lions.

Shortly before lunch I rang through to the Royal Hospital ground on Chelsea embankment to see if our Chelsea Casuals' strictly unadvertised game against the BBC had been called off. As usual the groundsman did not answer the telephone. He had a reputation for lurking among the trees and leaving the telephone to his wife. But his wife had rebelled. So it was a case of taking matters into one's own hands and going down to the ground to find him.

Our left-half had arrived early for the match, having one of those characteristic insatiable appetites for the game which minor Sunday footballers have. We went out into the rain. 'It can't be on,' I said. 'It's pissing.' 'Keep your finger crossed,' he said, squeezing a copy of *Ancient Chinese Philosophy* to his chest inside his raincoat. 'I've waited a week for this. It can't be off.' 'There isn't a chance,' I said, always a defeatist.

The suspense was awful. I suppose we knew already that the groundsman was waiting to tell us, rubbing his hands, that 'It's HOFF'. How many times had it happened at Hackney Marshes, Parliament Hill Fields and Hampstead Heath Extension. As our left-back had often said about Chelsea Royal Hospital: 'It only has to give a quick slash and that's it, the bastard.'

The rain had eased quite a bit by the time we reached the Embankment and turned right towards the ground. The

Thames flowed in streaks of dingy colour among the Battersea fringes. A youth wearing blue jeans and a cowboy hat with a cigarette hanging out of his mouth trudged past us with liquid streaming from his cast-iron ears. Through the gates of the Royal Hospital we saw the cannon balls piled beside those twin, ancient cannons, while the tall, phallic monument to Crimea dividing the two football pitches had buried itself in a greasy ceiling of low weather.

The pitch we had to play on, the smaller one on the right, was flooded with shallow pools of water, but not as much as the main pitch, were both goalmouths were swimming pools. We trudged, shoulders hunched with grief, along the path to the changing rooms. 'I can't stand it,' said the left-half.

Three figures stood outside the rickety hut which Chelsea Borough Council had the nerve to call a dressing room. They looked like grey herons in the rain, static and bloated with moisture.

I recognized the groundsman, a small, beaky-chinned man wearing a faded pinstriped suit, sodden and clipped at the ankles with bicycle clips. His hair was greased back so that the main movement occurred over the ears, two violent waves which roared back over the lobes leaving a thinning, calmer pool of hair on the top. His brown eyes protruded as if waiting for some signal which would shoot them out onto the path. His mouth was permanently open and as we ambled up he spoke in shrill cockney: 'It's HOFF.'

We backed away and then sideways as if to combat his statement and make him feel at ease so that he would change his mind. The two other men regarded him with sheer hate. The older one, just visible below a brown corduroy cap, was about thirty. His cheeks were flushed and chubby and there was hardly any mouth, a pink button through which an orange tongue occasionally flicked irritation. His shoulders were massive, his kneecaps prominent through a diarrhoea-coloured raincoat, his shoes Italian pointed, his eyes pig-like and red, probably from constant pints of bitter. His companion was younger and his corduroy cap, blue, was firmly planted over a greyhound-shaped snout. His body was lithe, his thin legs fixed to a pair of waterlogged brothel creepers.

Both men held onto small, leather suitcases, the older one having tied a football to his. 'It was the older one who spoke, his eyelashes fluttering like dragonflies. 'Did you hear him, did you hear him,' he said turning to us. 'He's joking. There's only a bit of piss out there and it says it's fucking hoff. Hoff. I'm telling yer we're playing.'

'It's hoff,' said the groundsman not giving away an inch. 'No play on pitch one today and no play on pitch two.'

The older player turned to us again and let his voice rise to a high pipe. 'I tell yer something,' he said. 'He's going to get done for this. Fuckin' well is.'

Our team had been overruled and we looked down mumbling that we might be able to play if the rain stopped. 'I'm telling you it's hoff. And when I say it's hoff, it's hoff. HOFF'

The younger player eased his way forward so he towered over the groundsman, whose smile hung like a cigarette butt on the edge of his mouth. 'We're playing the Wandsworth Sportsmen,' he said. 'Top of the league struggle. You can't put that fuckin' game off, honest to fuck you can't. I tell you we're going to put you in hospital, so'll the Sportsmen, you'll see. Fucking cheek.'

'It's hoff. Both games hoff. I called them hoff this morning. You should have rung like the other lads. They called and I said it's hoff, both team, both games, they didn't say anything. Stands to reason, look at it.'

'Fucking cheek,' said the older player.

The groundsman flung his chin at him. 'You've got any complaints speak to Chelsea Borough Council. They'll put you right. Go up and see 'em at the Town Hall tomorrow. Don't tell me what my job is. It's hoff.'

The two aggressors turned towards their pitch which was

now deeper under water, small air bubbles sending out tiny jets in the goalmouths. On the centre circle a tired group of pigeons pecked hopefully at a small, dry piece of island. But the sight of the two goal nets arranged in all their majesty, raindrops dripping from the rigging, made them squirm with irritation.

'Piss, it's only piss,' said the older one. 'You could play ten games on that and still have anuvver. I tell you something, Tich, you going to get done. Fuck the council, we'll do them too.'

'And a Wandsworth Sportsman will do 'em and you,' said the greyhound. 'The lads'll get you. A razor job, or you'll get a good thumping.'

'I know you lot,' said the grounds man. 'Always making trouble, bribing the ref, sorting out other lads. Well I'm telling you it's hoff. You can't threaten me. Nobody threatens me. I've had more war service than you've had hot dinners. The Burma campaign, it was.'

'Fuck Burma,' said the greyhound.

'We don't want nothing to do wiz Burma. We'll do you.'

'Fuck you,' said the older one giving the football attached to his suitcase a savage kick, thereby revealing the he was a thick-skinned full-back. He was still holding the suitcase so the effort took him five yards across the path and it looked almost ungainly.

'Fucker,' said the greyhound. 'You wait till the Wandsworth Sportsmen catch you. They'll be here soon.'

'They won't. They telephoned.'

'I couldn't get you.' I added meekly.

'Well, that's your bad luck,' said the groundsman. 'And your game's hoff too.' Thus ended our slim hopes that such aggression from the others would influence him to let us play.

'I've seen some fuck pigs in my life,' said the greyhound. He had pulled his cap down so that it perched on the end of his nose.

The older one pulled his shoulders back. 'I wouldn't be in your shoes, honest I wouldn't. You're going to get done.'

'See the Borough Council' said the groundsman.. 'It's hoff and now I'm hoff.' He pointed to a notice outside the dressing room door. 'See that.' It read, 'No Play Today'.

We hung around for another five minutes, but nobody came through the rain and nobody came from the Wandsworth Sports-men. All there was was the noise of the two players and the groundsman saying alternately" 'We'll have you, you cunt, we'll have you,' and 'It's hoff, hoff.'

The rain began to come down in rasping jets and the left-half said: 'Well that's it. Let's go back to your place.'

We walked moodily away down the path and could still hear the three men arguing and swearing. When we reached the gates of the Royal Hospital they were a blob of cantankerous human form far away beyond the drenched pitch number one.

'They'll still be there tomorrow,' said the left-half. We had to laugh.

X. Full-Backs

From tractors to Rolls Royces. The backs of today – Giacinto Facchetti of Inter Milan, and Karl Schnellinger, the blond West German left-back of A.C. Milan, to mention two, are the new aristocrats of the park. Not so long ago men of their standing were regarded as solid but unglamourous necessities.

The old honky-tonk era of full-backs is almost extinct in top football now, speedy, ball-playing backs go leap-frogging past their own wingers and shoot past the opposing goalkeeper as if they are natural centre-forwards. But it used to be quite different in circles where sweet soccer was supposed to be displayed.

As an example, Chelsea had a full-back after the war named Alec White. He was a massive fellow, very popular, with greasy black hair and shin guards the size of castle doors.

White was called 'Knocker' on the terraces of Stamford Bridge, because he got stuck in and got rid of the ball with a mighty boot. He was always 'good old Knocker'.

Knocker was typical of the breed of his day. If he had to kick the ball over the stand in an emergency he would endeavor to do so, although this at Chelsea was well nigh impossible even with thighs as well-endowed as his.

Chelsea took up a whole succession of full-backs like Knocker, and Mr Ted Drake, who came along later as manager, kept up the mood by employing two huge, inelegant backs in his championship side: Stanley Willemse and Peter Sillett.

Rather different from the stylishness of Eddie McCreadie, No. 3 at Stamford Bridge today. Strangely enough, it was Chelsea who included the Swiss inter-national full-back Willi Steffen in their line up during the 1946-47 season, apart from Johnny Carey, the first emancipated back to catch one's eye. Willi, a tall, refined player figured in a new system which surprisingly destroyed the great England side when they played Switzer-land in 1947. Basically the method, which became known as the Swiss, or double-bolt system, was that Steffen and the other back marked Tommy Lawton, the England centre-forward, while the centre-half covered the two inside forwards, and the wing-halves the wingers. The method in this match was a complete success and Switzerland won 1–0.

Willi's system was certainly not seen at Chelsea at that time, when the third-back game could not have been more conven-tional. There were a mass of large full-backs playing solidly square at this time and to watch Johnny Carey and Willi Steffen following the Eddie Hapgood constructive tradition was a rare delight.

It was an era when the teeth of opposing wingers littered the turf of Third Division grounds, and backs, catching pneu-monia from the severe draught from a passing foe, began panic clearances in all directions to the roar of 'Windy'. And nothing really mattered except to kick the ball away even if it meant knocking out the false teeth of the old man behind the goal or knocking off the hat of Martha Gobbles, charwoman, sta-tioned in the West stand enclosure.

Well you still get the panic stuff but it's rarer now and more surprising and even in the lower division of the thickest full-back has a go at bringing the ball upfield.

So tractors turn to Rolls Royces in the department of back and this has done the game no harm at all. The tradition of Eddie Hapgood, that sophisticated exponent of cultured play in the rear, borne on by Johnny Carey, Laurie Scott and George Hardwick, Roger Byrne and Bill Eckersley has now infiltrated into agricultural football.

We have seen modern masters since, like the mighty Santos pair, Djalma and Nilton, of Brazil's World Cup team, fitting gracefully into the 4-2-4 system, or linking defence and attack with subtle springy runs. And seen with approval a new pair of English backs, Cohen of Fulham, and Wilson of Everton, one a pacemaker on the right flank like his predecessor Jimmy Armfield, the other more defensive, less fast, but a stylish player.

In 4-2-4 the two backs flanking two centre-backs are expected to blanket the opposing wingers but also to use the ball to extent of running through on their own to centre or shoot. Speed is vital. Strong of Liverpool, a utility player and an experienced forward, has no difficulty in attuning himself to the right back position and spent much of his time going through to use his powerful shot. His goal against Juventus in the European Cup-winner Cup was a memorable effort. And count how often Lawler and Byrne, the regular backs come up for a poke.

In the 4-3-3 system it is hard to know who's got his name down the programme as a winger or a back because of all the leap-frogging going on and wingers coming back deep and backs going charging upfield. It does seem that positions on the field in the future will become even less departmental and the game will become as regimental and anonymous as pier football. While the back has become more sophisticated, other people on the field have lost their identity, especially on the wings.

Alf Ramsey, who doesn't believe in wingers any more, had a job at Tottenham which required stopping such rakish rogues such as Stanley Matthews, Tom Finney, and Peter Harris, who wouldn't have said they were anything else but wingers. Ramsey did an excellent job on countless occasions, a cultured right-back well ahead of his time.

The big boot was not for him, but it could never have

been the big boot in the Arthur Rowe's push-and-run side of 1950-51.

He instigated attacks from one of Ditchburn's quick throws and then away he would fly looking for Ron Burgess, or Sonny Walters, or Len Duquemin or Medley, his head boring down on over the ball as he ran, curly black hair like a black bush in the midst.

Alf's fault was being slow on the turn and a player like Blunstone of Chelsea often caught him off balance and left hum trundling behind, panting in failure.

And sometimes he could almost be too cultured, too relaxed as was the case when his back pass to Ditchburn in the 1953 Cup Semi-final never reached Ted but reached Mudie and landed up in the net. Ted screamed at Alf beating his hand on the ground and everyone said why didn't Alf kick the ball into the stands. But that wasn't Alf.

When it came to smooth running and accuracy you couldn't find a better player than Jim Langely of Fulham, who could make a corner, and he was a prodigious thrower, and come running mightily into the penalty area for a shot. Jim collected cigarette cards in his spare time, a cheerful man who always had a bad game against Brabrook of Chelsea but never reacted violently.

George Young, Sammy Cox, Tiger Shaw, Eiffel Tower-figures, who stood out in the Scottish team after the war, rugged players who came south to Wembley like visiting battleships.

Alf Sherwood and Wally Barnes were the same for Wales, and Carey and Alf McMichael for Ireland. They were indomitable figures, who often had to captain sides over-run by Matthews, Carter, Lawton, Mannion and Finney and Mortensen and the rest. But they played like men whose shirt meant everything to them. They were never disgraced.

XI. Upper Class

Soccer had never been a sport of the English rich until recently, when Lady H. discovered the game.

She discovered it through an intellectual, who was prone to stay long weekends at her country seat, whenever he could tear himself away from Stamford Bridge on Saturdays and playing the game himself in Hyde Park on Sunday mornings. Because he liked the game so much, Lady H. became intrigued, in the same way that her friends had taken to Pop Art, and one day she suggested to the intellectual that he bring his team, Battersea Park, down to her seat to play a side she would arrange from her own friends.

So Lady H. discovered the game, and I became one of those invited down to play for the intellectual's side, one wet, May Sunday. We were normally a scruffy lot on match days, turning up to play on London parks and recreation grounds with jeans and jerseys and black fingernails and a distinct facial flush which suggested Saturday nights ill-spent.

And so there we were that Sunday lunchtime, moving up the gravel drive of Lady H.'s magnificent eighteenth-century residence in a convoy of tiny cars and dressed in the same way and with the same flushes evident through each windscreen in blurs of pink. Lady H.'s residence, an incredible example of Georgian opulence, rose out of the rain in tiers of yellowish sponged limestone; shooting away on all sides were fountains spurting up into the blue misty atmosphere, beckoning mazes and tall box hedges all flowing on to surrounding woodland. On one side of the house was a majestic lake over which streaks of water from miniature fountains twinkled into the air. It was magical. 'What a bleeding manor,' said Norman, our resident wit and outside-right. 'Wouldn't mind a little place like this of me own. Look at that.'

A butler had come out onto the flight of steps leading into the house and taken our football tenderly from the hands of our intellectual. We got out of our cars and wandered vacantly across the gravel to the steps and climbed in a covey of indecisiveness towards the butler, dressed in black coat and striped trousers by the door.

The butler, who viewed our scruffiness with smiling tolerance invited us to leave our gear in the main hall. Then the delightful, fresh-faced Lady H. swept forward and we all shook hands and sniffed the warm smell of leather, old wood and old masters and Lady H.'s soft perfume.

She said, 'Marvellous to meet you – all of you.'

Then we were summoned into a vast dining room lined with paintings by Van Dyck, where a selection of sumptuous delights such as cold turkey and chicken were laid out for our use with jugs of wine-cup to wash the food down. Martin, our outside-left, asked the butler rather nervously for a glass of beer and the butler said, 'Certainly sir' and came back with a crate of bottles. 'Watch it, Martin,' I said, 'or you'll be missing the far post.'

Scattered around the long table were members of the opposing team, eyeing us with mild amusement, big, muscular young men in sports jackets whom we assumed, quite rightly as their laughter hooted towards the ceiling, to be in the main, merchant bankers.

Lady H. was in tremendous form, garrulous and generous, and full of soccer. She announced rather anxiously as we dug into her food, that the gardeners had spent the previous day laying out the pitch, and she hoped it would be the right size and that the goal-posts cut down by steaming foresters from a nearby wood would be the right shape and size. Opposite me was one of the most beautiful girls I had ever seen, with green, metallic eyes and a soft smirk hovering on the corners of her exquisite mouth. I examined her, stimulated by the wine cup, but just as I was about to catch her attention a corpulent young man with thin steel glasses made a hearty remark next to me.

'Hullo Danny Blanchflower. We're going to massacre you today. You haven't a chance. Ho, ho, ho.' Our team looked suitably brazen and all stuck out our chins in defiance. 'Who's Danny Blanchflower?' wheezed the girl.

'A footballer,' I said.

'Oh,' she said. 'Is he marvelous?'

Lady H. rose from the table with a sound which suggested birds rising in a voluminous mass into the sky. This youngish woman was already obsessed with the thought of an afternoon of soccer, while we ageing men, mulled by the wine cup and rich food, were certainly not.

Usually we played our football in the mornings after a rushed cup of coffee, and we played in the surroundings less awe-inspiring and calming than these, so at that moment we were not at all fit for combat.

'Do let's start,' said Lady H. So we reluctantly got to our feet amid gusts of laughter from the merchant bankers.

Another beautiful woman appeared, who was pregnant and married to one of the opposition. She again had that calming, windblown appearance which rich women have and she instantly and easily took over the scene as much as the younger girl and Lady H.

The butler led us upstairs to a line of bedrooms and we were invited to strip. White towels were laid out, as thick as walls, and the butler motioned that if there was anything we wanted, to ring him. What a reverse of the man I had got to know so well in Sunday football – the gruff, unyielding, often rude LCC park keeper.

These conditions to change in were quite out of context

with Hackney Marshes dressing rooms or Wormwood Scrubs and it was pleasing to crouch on a soft eiderdown rather than on a hard bench. Stripped, Martin and I stood there on the soft carpet in our flashy socks and black strip, popped in the usual gum and made for the hall.

Under a blueish Canaletto, the butler was holding the football, the match ball, a blank look on his face.

'Your ball, sir,' he said to the intellectual, who took it with suitable aplomb.

Outside on the terrace we put on our boots, which crunched along the gravel. The girls had joined the advancing mob, wearing black cloaks. Lady H. had decided to referee the fracas and wore a long skirt down to her ankles and a simple pink shirt and her hair up in a bun.

The scene was pure Rousseau, in particular his painting 'The Players', with striped, ancient footballers dancing long-toed with a ball. Bordering the narrow pitch were dark, sinister shrubs and, at the far end, perched on an uplift of terrace, a gracious, antique summer house.

The ground was a fair size, although hardly big enough for sixteen brutes and two dwarfs who padded onto the pitch with Lady H. leading, chin in the air, saying, 'Ready, ready'. The two dwarfs were her sons of prep school size, wearing black jerseys which tickled their ankles and hung in sleeve-length down to their knees.

They had been conscripted to keep goal at each end and what I saw in the eyes of at least one of them was washy reluctance. Lady H. gave us Charles, a bumptious lad with hair like Billy Foulke, the Chelsea goalkeeper of pre-First World War, who weighed twenty-two stone, and banged the heads of opposing forwards together. Charles' hairstyle had the same urchin appearance but there the similarity ended.

Cold, black clouds scudded across the trees, the breeze hissed through Lady H.'s sacred shrubs, as we self-consciously kicked a ball about and watched our opponents standing hands in pockets smoking filter tips.

Lady H. called up the captains, and our Tony almost cracked her fair hand when he shook her palm. I had time to see the two girls standing outlined in black against the skyline, their hoods transforming them each into devils from the Seventh Seal, before kicking off.

I had hardly played the ball away when I found myself lying on the ancient turf breathing in short gulps. Above me was a corpulent merchant banker, his breath smelling of wine cup, his mouth hanging open in mild amusement, his cheeks smears of pink toothpaste.

'So it's going to be like that is it, you bastard.'

Lady H. hadn't blown and like a wild pack of hounds her team thundered down on our nervous goalkeeper who turned his back on the ball and let it trickle gently into the goal. As far as could be seen nobody had actually put the ball in the net, although the goal counted. Lady H. blew her whistle with great panache and pointed towards her navel thereby signalling a goal. There were hoots of delight from the girls down the other end and the girl who wasn't pregnant let her hood slip back off her hair and blowing out her lips bawled: 'Splendid.'

'Shit,' said Tony below his breath. 'Come lads. Let's start playing.'

It became that sort of game with goals every two minutes and both sides moving on from 3-3 to 6-6 with every shot going in and the tackles getting harder and harder and blood on knees and Lady H. blowing her whistle so the noise poured away shrilly across the countryside, so that rooks were disturbed and pigeons cooed. The tackling became so ferocious that only the most ungentlemanly measures could combat them. This was not a pleasant afternoon in the country, it was soccer the aristocratic way.

When Martin was brought down by Christopher, a sallow attractive boy with a Beatles haircut and fine pink linen shorts, just before half time, Lady H. blew her whistle for a penalty.

I approached this task with saliva sticking to the edges of my mouth and a dirty look in my eye. Normally, for Lady H.'s sake, I would have treated this kick with all the courtesy which her hospitality afforded, but the opposition had now enflamed me so much that I decided to take the kick as if I was facing Frank Swift.

Ahead, Lady H.'s son went down on his knees and grimaced at me with such a look of loathing that I hit the ball into the corner of the goal with all my strength; it licked up a row of small shrubs, bounced against a grey wall and puffed its way into the trees. 'That's the way. Let's batter them,' said Michael as I was hugged Spurs-fashion by my colleagues.

At half-time Tony picked up a dead starling in the summer house and held it as if he was clutching a cup of tea in a First Division dressing room. We were still losing 10-11. 'Come on, lads,' he said moodily, stroking the feathers of the bird.

'What a marvellous game,' said Lady H. 'You're all doing frightfully well.' As she spoke horrifying claps of thunder and liquid lightning engulfed us so that the tall trees swayed like giants looking down on us with scorn. Rain pinged on the roof of the summerhouse and we prepared to wait half an hour for the weather to abate.

But Lady H. summoned us out onto the field again, and by some freak chance in the darkness I found myself playing against my own side and one of them playing for us. When the light grew better it was decided to keep it that way and goal after goal continued to go and Lady H. blew and blew and bones crunched and crunched, and then Martin smashed in a shot on the volley and it caught Lady H. on the jaw. She went down like a log, a bundle of pink, her face streaming with rain, her bun a waterlogged hedgehog, her faint lipstick lost inside a panting mouth.

We all lifted her up and by that I mean all of us struggled and fought to get her up and the rain continued to pour down. The girls came tiptoeing through the mud and stood over her calling out 'Bunny, Bunny, how ghastly.'

'Better stop it,' said Tony.

'Nonsense,' said Lady H., opening her eyes. 'I'm perfectly all right. Let's carry on.' She rose and blew hard and long on her whistle and again we rushed into each other without care for science, without care for all we had seen and observed and been educated with by watching professional football. The only thing to do was to kick the ball as hard as you could at goal and it would usually go in and there would be the battered but unbeaten Lady H. pointing to her navel and signaling a goal. In the end I think her side and now my side made it by 18-17 but it didn't really matter by then.

'Tea,' said Lady H., blowing full time. Tony kicked the ball into a nearby fountain and we all sloped off with our wounds. 'What a splendid game,' said a merchant banker flicking off a piece of mud from his green pants. His eyes glistened with pleasure through his steel-rimmed glasses. The party filed back to the house and the butler motioned us back to our rooms where we wallowed in hot baths and shoved great lashings of talcum powder on our pubic hairs and armpits and rubbed eau de cologne into our bruises and made ourselves stink.

'We didn't use the long ball enough,' said the intellectual. 'Next time we come up here we'd better win.'

'Who cares,' said Tony.

'Well I do,' said the intellectual.

We had tea with Canaletto, surrounded by blues and Venetian landscapes and gondolas and people locked in colour. The tea was real tea and cakes as large as mortar bombs. The girl who wasn't pregnant sat opposite me with a look of amused detachment on her face, 'It was terribly funny,' she said.

'It was tough.'

'We laughed and laughed.'

Lady H. arrived dressed in simple Chanel pink and ready for tea, her teeth flashing, a sparkle in her eye, her bun now abandoned for fine long streaky brown hair. 'You must, must all come down again,' she said. 'We'll win, next time,' said the intellectual politely but secretly hating the result.

'We did take our chances,' hooted the merchant banker down the table. Christopher flicked back his Beatle haircut and gave a long sorrowful glance down the table towards the girl who wasn't pregnant. She caught it for a moment, held it without expression and with a vague jerk of her chin flung it back again. 'They must be having an affair,' I thought.

Lady H. said she had been delighted to see us and gave us cocktails before we left for London. The girl who was pregnant and her husband became hearty members of the party dispelling fine, regal looks as well as drinks and they even managed to cheer up the intellectual who had become very depressed because we had lost. We all sat around on sofas and the girl, who wasn't pregnant smiled occasionally and said she was looking for a modeling job, or if she couldn't get one she would go to Corfu. Lady H. said how thrilled she was with the game and she had not suffered unduly from Martin's shot. For next time, she said, she would buy proper goalposts and nets. About seven, we all filed out onto the drive and got into our little cars and drove away.

As the huge house receded into pale, pastel shadows washed by rainwater, and an orange sunset formed in thin slices behind the turrets, the intellectual's face curled up again in anger.

'We needn't have lost the bloody thing.'

XII. Fulham: Craven Cottage

There's a laugh waiting in my belly whenever I go to the Fulham Football Ground, which is called Craven Cottage. It begins at Putney Bridge Station, or on Putney Bridge where the buses stop, and it is ready to burst out into the chilly air at any time on the walk through Bishops Park by the grey Thames where Victoriana drips sweat from leafy trees washed by the rain.

And the laugh comes out near the bandstand in Bishops Park, where a pissed crowd of West Ham supporters have assembled singing 'We're forever blowing bubbles'. And and old Fulham lag cries 'We're beat the bleeding lot of you by two penalties to one penalty'. And the West Ham supporters start dancing with each other on the stand and making obscene gestures.

Fulham are a Saturday afternoon team. There is always a feeling of animated recreation rather than solid professionalism about the scene, so that girls playing on tennis courts near the ground, with elephantine thighs, on which hang white slips seemingly made of Kleenex and playing strokes off their chins, appear almost part of the football game itself. And there is a feeling of the past, with the rows and rows of Victorian houses from which old men stare through stained glass eyes of Saint Peter and Saint Paul.

Get yourself a hot dog. Here is Craven Cottage in the rain with the wind drifting across the banks of the Thames on the popular side, blowing dinghies downstream so that their masts wobble above the advertising boards and the half-time score board which nobody can understand.

Buy yourself a programme. It was quite in order to read in a Fulham programme the other day about a remedy for high blood pressure, 'the natural remedy', and of course Fulham Football Club must have noted that their often frustrated fans needed this advertisement.

Craven Cottage is a pretty ground which was once the home of Bulwer Lytton, and where he wrote *The Last Days of Pompeii*, a point often used by tired journalists to fill up space. Now the cottage itself, a bricked-box with a balcony, where hangers on and the privileged have a peep at the game. And where the players change and have a drink after the game.

The flags of First Division Clubs flutter in the wind on the river-side of Craven Cottage, and the cranes dip their heads in salutation, when Fulham take the field, spreading out onto the pitch, Johnny Haynes biting his lip and, head down, contemplating his knee caps.

The actual playing opponents of Fulham Football club are always supremely polite when they play at Craven Cottage, and if they achieve total victory they leave the field blushing and rubbing the wet heads of the home-side in commiseration.

The opposing manager falls over himself to congratulate Fulham for their brave fight under difficult conditions, how nobly Haynes and his lads fought unsuccessfully to square the one goal penalty they lost by.

On the other hand, if Fulham beat the league leaders, as was the case against Liverpool in February 1966, when themselves at the bottom of the league, the opposition can disintegrate into eleven inmates of the padded cell with a provoked centre-forward named Ian St. John making a final gesture by felling Mark Pearson with a left hook as clean and beautiful as one exploited by Sugar Ray Robinson at Madison Square Garden.

Elsewhere this wouldn't seem very funny, but at Craven Cottage Ian St. John's indignant march to the dressing room seemed merely another piece of grotesque comedy on a ground made for the zany activities of the Keystone Cops.

Since the War, I have seen Fulham transfer from a side of humourless efficiency watched by humourless, patriotic spectators, who were always cynical of the music hall comedians of Stamford Bridge, to a side of happy, sometimes comic triers watched by garrulous actors who detest the thorough efficiency of the now highly organized Stamford Bridge set up.

In 1949 they won the Second Division Championship by one point, from West Bromwich Albion, with the help of a feast of goals from Arthur Rowley, Jack Rowley's brother, Bedford Jezzard, who later became an England forward and manager of the club, and right-winger Arthur Stevens, who used to run, hands dangling in front of him.

The side did not last in the First Division and they were relegated in 1952. But the arrival of Johnny Haynes in the first team added the spice from which the side came back again in 1959 and round him were players like Jimmy Hill, his beard cantering after a through ball, centre half Roy Bentley, who had come from Chelsea, a spectacular goalkeeper, Tony Macedo, the long-legged, always willing left-back Jim Langley, Eddie Lowe, bald and profuse at left half, the sharp-shooting Scot, Graham Leggat, and Arthur Stevens, still there as he had always been, running.

There were great moments, including the Cup run of 1958, when, mainly through Macedo's errors in the semi-final replay at Highbury, Fulham were eliminated by Manchester United and Bobby Charlton. But the side recently has not had an easy time in the First Division, and a number of close escapes culminated in the Houdini effort at the end of the 1966 season when they took 19 points from 12 games and survived.

When Vic Buckingham first made his appearance as manager of Fulham in 1965, he found an atmosphere of the friendliness, of cosiness, and, on the bad side, a feeling of almost cocky nonchalance; like a man laughing at an envelope he knows encloses news of a hideous overdraft and doesn't dare open it.

He tightened up discipline, made the Fulham players break into rather more than a mild pre-cocktail canter, but Fulham continued to lose. As a last card desperately thrown, Johnny Haynes was switched to a deep lying No. 9 position and it worked. Haynes, helped by the sheer professionalism of Bobby Robson, Graham Leggat and George Cohen, steered the club clear assisted by the coaching of Dave Sexton, who had arrived on the eve of a miracle.

For some years this Fulham projector has been showing very funny films. But they have all seemed part of the pleasant scenery, part of the show business stage. This was not surprising because there are people around Craven Cottage who were not fitted to the sheer, bluff professionalism of other clubs.

You could say the club was unconventional, with the comedian Tommy Trinder as chairman, and bandleader Chappie D'Amato as a director, whose band I have seen the tiny breasts of debutantes go all a fluttering to a rendering of, 'I could have danced all night,' and a blonde centre-half in Bobby Keetch, who enters Wheeler's in Soho dressed in an Edwardian overcoat with a girl covered in oil skin, and greeted by the manager saying: 'Your table, Mr Keetch,' and Bobby talking about Pop Art and not football.

It seemed part of the comic scene when there was a tall, lanky kid with curly hair called Maurice Cook, who took his goals well but always ran with a slightly awkward look as if he was a stork in the process of taking off. Then there was an outside left, called Tosh Chamberlain, who once sent in a shot at his own goal with such force that it almost broke Tony Macedo's ribs. Well Tosh could always break the net at the other end too, but sometimes he forgot which way he was going.

In the middle of all this Johnny Haynes has remained like one of the lions in Trafalgar Square, ignoring all the giggles around him, the provider of the most beautiful reverse passes in England since the war, defense cutters as lethal as steel shears, a man of many moods who survived injuries, was hated in the North where he was regarded as the golden boy of the hated South. This came about when he became the first £100-a-week footballer under the new deal. But he deserved it – Fulham's greatest player.

Haynes is the hero of the showbusiness crowd. See them flock to the Cottage to watch 'Johnny'; serious actors, pantomime players, bandleaders, stunt men, starlets, dressed up in frenzied casual clothes, tweeds, black leather, green leather, pink ankle-length knickers, starched blue jeans, baggy overcoats over armour-plated suede jackets, toy revolvers in their pockets, cheroots between thumb and first finger.

'There's Cathy Gale without the leather,' shouts a voice. They bring their loud voices and their loyalty to the enclosure and after-wards, invade Sean Treacy's Queen Elm Pub, in the Fulham Road, where Fulham are always 'great', even if they have been dismal, and Danny Blanchflower, talking to Bob Ferrier of *The Observer* about golf, is prodded by ten fingers and told: 'Fulham were great, weren't they, Danny, great?' 'We were Great,' 'A bit bizarre,' says Danny.

The congregation, dressed like mountain hares, stamp their fur boots on the floor of the pub and are not convinced. 'Come off it, Danny. We were unlucky.' 'We've hit the upright seven times this month.' Johnny Haynes strides into the pub and is encircled by admirers. He smiles over to Blanchflower as one insider to another. They murmur a few words to each other about the ill-fortunes of the afternoon.

Johnny has a light ale and listens to the showbusiness crowd dissecting the game. He is a polite listener and adds his own thoughts and criticism, when the conversation threatens to run too much into one-sided patriotism.

'That kid's a natural but he ruins it by doing stupid things,' says Johnny.

Bobby Keetch comes in and the conversation switches

from football to Op Art and birds, but Danny Blanchflower is still talking to Bob Ferrier about golf. There is a sudden howl of laughter as an actor tells a dirty story about the Kop. Annie Ross, the jazz singer sits on a stool and tells you, with her bright eyes pushing out below a fur hat, that 'it was a groovy game. But a real shame, we should have won.'

The game is over and one thinks back to the game and the slightly comic way in which Fulham threw it away. But we had a lot of laughs.

I first laughed at Fulham after the war when a fat goalkeeper came rushing at me, parallel to the ground, before hitting the back of the net, his head wedged by a stanchion. The goalkeeper had been charged into the net by an opposing forward as he went to collect a centre and he hit the net so hard that steam rose from his jersey. As he struggled cursing in the net with the ball wedged between his knees, the man who sent him there mocked him before running back to the centre-circle with his colleagues gnawing at his neck in appreciation.

The goalkeeper's two full-backs picked him up and brushed him down and looked to see if he had lost any teeth, but he didn't have many anyway, and the goalkeeper cursed the forward and shouted at the ref who was standing immobile pointing up at the cranes leaning above the terrace at the other end of the ground to signal a goal.

'My bloody feet were off the ground, ref,' said the goalkeeper. 'He hit me, the bogger, with my feet off the ground.' But it was a goal all right and the ref walked back smiling to the centre circle.

'Did you see the bogger, he hit me feet off the ground,' turning to us standing behind the net. He was still muttering when he was beaten by a shot from twenty yards into the top corner.

'Bogger,' said the keeper. 'Wasn't the bogger a yard offside.'

It happened one day at Craven Cottage, where Bulwer Lytton wrote *The Last Days of Pompeii*.

XIII. Pele

It was the summer in Paris when General de Gaulle came back to power – a Sunday in June 1958, when the city was trying uneasily to get back to normal after the national crisis.

I awoke in my Left Bank hotel, with a hangover which formed a red mist when I opened my eyes. There was a thumping sensation above my right eye and odd flashes sped to and fro in the mind recalling the previous night, which had started with an extraordinary reception for the Moscow Arts Theatre at the Russian Embassy and finished up in broad daylight on the Champs Elysees. Thump, thump, thump, the World Cup Final in Stockholm today, where can I watch it on television, oh not a bar, not another cognac, no more cognac.

The telephone rang above my head – a shrill purr which made every nerve scream. 'Hullo, hullo, oh hullo Laura, I've been meaning to ring you. Congratulations. I couldn't believe it. Louis told me when I was leaving London. What a surprise.'

Laura spoke fast and feverishly after my early splutterings. 'How is Louis, oh, how is he? I'm feeling so depressed without him. The engagement has made me feel sick. I feel quite sick.'

'It's mutual.'

'Why?'

'Well, I'm not engaged or in love but I have a terrible hangover. Can we meet later. I've got something for you from Louis.'

'Oh yes, please, please. Where? Look I'm on expenses here. Pick me up at my hotel, at the Continental, at two and you can tell me everything then. Bye.'

The telephone went down with a click and it was seconds before I realized my mistake, The World Cup Final between Sweden and Brazil would be due at that time. I had been planning to sneak off and see it in some quiet hotel lounge. Oh, hell. I was going to miss the final and it promised to be a great final. Sweden had reached it with a sustained display of busy football, but Brazil, particularly in the semi-final against France, had been in a mood where genius is rarely far away and often exposed in waves of sheer majesty.

I had watched earlier rounds in London and was determined to see the final somehow. But Laura who had just got engaged to a friend, looked like putting an end to it. Normally it would have been a lunch to run to, and on expenses too, but that morning I dressed gingerly and reluctantly. Stymied.

Laura, a tall, warm, gangling blonde was waiting for me at her hotel, and I pressed a fading red rose from Louis into her palm. Then she was eagerly asking about how Louis was and how he looked and how he felt about being engaged to her. As we ambled along the Rue de Rivoli in the sunshine, with the Paris traffic purring past like a mountain stream on the other side of the arches, I began the discreet task of saying how grandiose and special Louis was and how he was missing her and missing her so much that he had called me every hour at my office to say how much he was missing her.

Laura said: 'Terrific,' sticking the rose into a buttonhole.

We walked on until we reached a restaurant area, but they were all select and expensive, full of cakes and sour women and we avoided them almost automatically. What I was trying to find without actually saying so was a restaurant with a television set.

At last we came to a pretentious joint with yellow umbrellas outside and a bourgeoisie look which would make any Michelin-conscious person run a mile. The whole place smelt of a tourist trap with menus outside in English, German and Japanese and there was a sign above the door, COME IN.

But inside the restaurant I caught sight of a television set on a ledge, just near the table, and it was on and jittering. 'Here we are,' I said to Laura knowing she wasn't much of a gourmet. 'Let's try this.'

Laura nodded dreamily, miles away anyway. She was most certainly in love, a small smile hovering on the corner of her mouth, her left hand hitting at objects as if they were passing splendours of a summer landscape and she was pushing them aside along her stroll.

We went in and sat down in the restaurant and the fat proprietor came forward grinning at us suckers. There was a heavy pink feeling about the place, the paint was pink, the proprietor's face was pink and even the salads on the other tables looked vaguely pink. We were given enormous menus and the prices, on first inspection, were enormous.

Laura looked at hers, cooing *oeuf mayonnaise* and *entrecote* through the two palms she had hung her chin on and I followed along the *oeuf mayonnaise* but settled for chicken.

'Are you putting the match on,' I said to the proprietor.

'*Oui, Monsieur.*'

Glory, glory, my heart thumped and the view was perfect, the set placed a few yards behind Laura's shoulder blades. She was nibbling an olive. 'What match?'

'Oh, the World Cup Final. It might be nice to watch it later.'

'Well you can. Now tell me about Louis.'

I told her about him and how handsome he looked and how they should have got together because it was so obvious they were suited to each other. And what a great wedding it was going to be. And Louis was sending love and more love and since the engagement he couldn't do anything but sit in his flat playing rock 'n' roll records, mumbling to himself and looking at the ceiling, wrapped up in a grey towelling dressing gown with streaks of whiskey across the knees.

I tried to enrich her as much as possible as she sat looking across at me with a gentle smile on her face occasionally uttering a sigh and tickling her snub nose with her knuckles so that I felt myself falling for her a bit myself.

We had got through the *oeuf mayonnaise* and the clock was nearing the zero hour at Stockholm. I thought of Brian Glanville and other journalists I knew who must by now be in their seats, Brian giving the pitch one of those long, fierce, perceptive stares he sometimes does before a game.

'I feel sick,' said Laura.

'Why?'

'Louis. I can't stand it, I really can't. Since I arrived on Thursday I haven't been able to think. I think I'll have to give up this job. It's going to be impossible.'

Laura had got a good job as a secretary to an American journalist. She was very bright, and would probably do much more, especially in the television line where she had experience. 'I should stay on for a bit,' I said. 'Three months anyway.'

'I can't when I feel sick all the time.' She looked down at her *entrecote* with disgust. 'Oh God. This thing inside me. This love thing.'

She got up and walked away towards the toilet and I wondered if she was pregnant. No, it was probably love. Laura had always been a highly emotional girl. The television set flashed on the Eurovision sign and now through sudden lines and fluttering flags appeared in the Rasunda Stadium at Stockholm. I looked round the dining room and other men paused over their food to watch.

We might have been there, our mouths hung open waiting as the teams lined up and the French commentator began to en-flame the room with possible tactics and forecasts. The Brazilian players looked so elastic as they kicked about and there was the smooth figure of Didi, who had smashed the French in the semi-final.

Laura came back and sat down. 'Oh,' she said, looking at the set, 'that' and 'Oh' again. I nodded smiling nervously.

'How do you feel?'

'Oh, so I wasn't sick. Silly really. Go on about Louis.'

So I went on about Louis, but as I talked about Louis I kept my eyes on the set behind her and pushed chicken up to my mouth without really thinking. I wasn't hungry and the hangover hadn't gone. But the wine, a cold rose, was good and we had a lot of it.

The game had got off to a sumptuous start which helped even my description of Louis. I described how I had first met him at a London party and how the sight of him standing like a handsome heavyweight champion holding a glass of Scotch on the rocks had convinced me that here was a man who was going to be seen around for a long time to come.

'He seemed highly intelligent, easy going but not smooth. I was – GOAL . . .'

Laura was shaken by my rude change of pace. Within five minutes Liedholm had put the ball in the Brazilian net after a neat movement between Bergmark, Borjesson and Simonsson. This was a surprise and men in the restaurant visibly shook over their *saucisson a l'ail*.

'Oh, sorry. Sweden have gone ahead. At any rate Louis has impeccable taste in clothes. Oh, look at that.'

I had lost my composure. Brazil, with Garrincha flashing down the right wing, were forcing their way into the game. I tried to talk more about Louis, but the game was winning and Louis was definitely losing. I could think only of Louis's bad points. His bad temper and irresponsibility. I almost revealed them without thinking and then, 'GOAL' – Garrincha leapt away from Axbom like a tiger, and came wiggling up the bye line and Vava smashed the ball in (1-1). Our companions nodded their heads in the restaurant as if this was inevitable.

More and more we saw Garrincha and more and more Pele, darting and dawdling and flashing forward. '*Ohhhh*,' Pele's shot, a left footer curled against a Swedish post and came out.

'Marriage worries me,' said Laura abstractedly. 'I've never really thought about it before. It is rather terrifying.'

'But it is a good thing you are so certain. Oh GOAL, what a GOAL.' From Pele to Didi, the cobra, a flash of Garrincha again, and Vava had hammered in another goal (2-1).

'I never knew you liked football,' said Laura dreamily.

'Oh, but I do.'

We sat now over our coffee and cognac and we were both far away, Laura with Louis, and I with Pele and Garrincha and the rest who were now playing a brand of football one sees only two or three times in a lifetime.

The white ball was being stroked and manoeuvered by brilliant individualists, and at the same time they were still very much a streamlined squad, a team.

Every contemptuous gesture which covered an individual, spectacular movement, was followed by a decisive pass which brought the Brazilian team nearer the Swedish goal. The Swedes toiled gallantly but they were being outclassed.

After half-time Laura was content to let me watch the game while she sat smiling into her coffee cup. I was happy she was happy and happy to be watching Brazil. The other diners in the restaurant included two very large sweating men who sat swaying with wonder as the Swedish defence was shattered over and over again.

Ten minutes after half-time came a goal in which Pele became not so much a member of the Brazilian team but a genius of the future. From Zagallo's cross, he played a little game of his own with the ball, with his instep, before flicking it over Gustavsson and banging home the ball like a bullet. (3-1). One of the large men choked. '*Bravo, Bravo, tres joli.*'

We drank our coffee and men in the restaurant caught each other's eyes and nodded and shuddered with pleasure. Simonsson scored a lovely goal to make the score 4-2 but Pele was now unstoppable and his header from Zagallo went swishing into Svensson's net. We stood up and applauded as the Brazilian players brushed the ball to each other with tender concern. Laura said: 'I'm going back to London. It's no good.

I must see Louis.'

When the match came to an end, and the Brazilian players made a victory run round the pitch with the trophy, we sat back and basked astonishment in the summer sunshine pouring through the windows of the restaurant. This had been a game which would rarely be repeated. We felt almost pompous and two large sweating men swallowed their cognacs so that the liquid trickled down their chins.

'*BRAVO.*'

We had seen a new Matthews in Garrincha, with a devastating burst, and a lethal youngster in Pele, and Didi again shrewd and magnificent in midfield, and Gylmar in goal, safe and acrobatic, the massive Bellini at centre half and the deadly Vava at centre-forward. These and the rest had been incredible.

Laura sat rubbing her knuckles against her chin that afternoon in Paris in 1958 as the proprietor turned off the television and gave us a big satisfied smile as if he was going to double the bill for all of us because of Pele.

The bill in fact was enormous but Laura paid without thinking, flopping down a ten thousand franc note with a yawn. 'I'm going back, she said. 'I can't stay away from Louis. It's impossible.'

'I'm going back to London tomorrow,' I said. 'Why don't you wait on a few days and I'm sure Louis will join you. You can't throw up a good job like this. It will keep you thinking until the wedding instead of mooning around Chelsea.'

'Oh no, no. I've got to go.'

One of the large and sweating men got up, rubbed his enormous stomach and the belt that lolled forwards towards his knees and ambled towards us. '*Monsieur, avez vous vu Pele? Magnifique.*' He belched and walked on out of the restaurant.

We got up and walked out into the late afternoon sunshine. I had Pele on my mind and Laura had Louis. We strolled along without talking for about a quarter of a mile and then Laura went into her hotel. I kissed her on the cheek and thanked her for the lunch and she thanked me for telling her about Louis. She said she would telephone me tomorrow if she was still in Paris.

I walked over to the Left Bank and bought a copy of *France Soir* which carried the World Cup half time score. It was loaded with surprise about Sweden's early lead. I looked forward to the later editions and Geoffrey Green's report in *The Times* the next day.

Laura did leave for London the next day, a few hours before me and she threw up her job into the bargain. But she never married Louis. It was another of those things.

XIV. Wing-Halves

Whenever the mind puts on a film show of twenty years of football, in the bath, or on the District Line, or in a Manchester taxi, one of the big stars is invariably Duncan Edwards, the left-half of England and Manchester United, who was killed in the Munich air disaster.

To recall him is to recall a massive lad with a Midlands accent who seemed literally to fill the field of play with his exuberance and power. To recall the days when he moved up field in the red shirt of Manchester United, or the white shirt of England, like a Brooklyn cab driver tackling the Manhattan traffic, is to recall more than a player with a long international future already secure.

Edwards in the memory is more than that, more than a mere player with strength in his legs and fire in his belly. He appears on the screen as an artist of genius, so persuasive is the vision that one can still see a trace of mud clinging to his white shorts on one particular afternoon, the souvenir of an explosive advance on the opposing goal.

And the movie show recalls that afternoon at Highbury, in February 1958, when Matt Busby's youthful side made their last appearance on an English ground before the Munich crash shattered them. Edwards comes to view as a huge giant in all-white strip bounding through a match won by Manchester United 5-4, after a noble Arsenal revival, but United always showed during the game that they could put the pressure on when they wanted to, and Edwards ran the motor.

It was Edwards who put United ahead with a goal in the first half which seared over the mud from 25 yards out and beat Jack Kelsey, a man not often beaten from that distance, through sheer speed.

Edwards won eighteen caps for England but they would probably have gone to a hundred. No side admired him more than Real Madrid, who knocked out Manchester United in the European Cup semi-finals of 1957, with Alfredo di Stefano and Raymond Kopa. They were the more experienced side and deserved the success which was to lead them to winning the trophy once again. But they would have liked to have had Edwards.

People are always talking about Edwards. A random incident told recently by a friend: 'I was standing behind the net at St James' Park,' he said, 'and Scoular came forward and hit a corner kick on the volley about fifteen yards from goal. He got the full meat of his boot behind the ball and it moved towards Wood like one of Napoleon's cannon balls at Borodino. Duncan stood there and headed the ball away with no effort at all and it went straight out to his left winger. It looked so easy that nobody appreciated just what he had done, but if it had hit anybody else it would have knocked their head off.'

Few people could unleash the cross-pass to the opposite wings with the proficiency of Edwards or soar through the middle for a shot at goal with players bouncing off him as if they were drops of rain falling on a whale.

Generally British half-backs have not been rare in quality since the War. Indeed the players who have worn the Number 4 and 6 shirts for England, Scotland, Wales and Ireland make up a profuse school of exceptional talent. To begin with we had players like Ronnie Burgess of Wales and Spurs, a balding, fiery attacking player and scorer of many an outrageous goal, who, when Tottenham started their push-and-run era, deliberately modified his approach by cutting down his dribbling in favour of quick 20-yard passing thus keeping his defence in a tighter position and getting his forwards on top of the opposition before they could draw breath; Joe Mercer of Arsenal, a defensive professor in a championship side; Bobby Evans, the cultured red-haired Celtic and Scotland half-back; Henry Cockburn of England, a tenacious little ferret from Ashton-under-Lyme. Archie Macaulay of Arsenal and Scotland, always creating, and of course Jimmy Dickinson of Portsmouth and England, an exquisite passer of the ball. And then in later years Danny Blanchflower of Spurs and Ireland, a player who seemed to crouch, shielding the ball as he moved upfield, as if to disguise its very presence from the opposition and then slanting it away to a square of least resistance, a garrulous native of Belfast. The Spurs players appreciated Danny because he was such a masterful reader of a game. He might have been overbearing theoretically but you don't win the double by having a dunce as a captain. And then there was Danny's No. 6, the swashbuckling Dave Mackay, who smashed the opposition in the Edwards manner by refusing to be knocked off the ball, even when hit by a steam engine. It cost him dear, eventually, with two broken legs and now his performance has lost that supreme bite and he tends to give up more easily when a game is going against Spurs. But in full flight Dave was one of the great half-backs.

And now we have Bobby Moore in the England side, a smooth, streamlined young Londoner with the appearance of a male model, whose methods have been built for the new emancipated soccer of 4-2-4 and 4-3-3. Moore is happiest as a defensive player moving laterally as a sweeper up behind his defence. I have often felt that he has neglected his attacking qualities which are undoubtedly there although recently he has not always shown up well when given this freedom for England. But Moore can be deadly when he suddenly switches from defence and swings a devastating through ball to an unmarked forward. I remember his mud-caked form breaking out of his own penalty area in the Cup semi-final between West

Ham and Manchester United, sweeping past two United players on the touch line and then sending Hurst away to score the all important goal.

And to mention a few more who are with us now, Nobby Stiles, a navvy with legs made of pickaxes, of Manchester United and England, who is one of the perpetual motion footballers of the sixties; Billy Bremner of Leeds, who ought to be called 'The Heavy Metal kid' from William Burroughs' *Nova Express*. These two players get into knocks and disorders through sheer exuberance, especially Bremner, but the game needs them now like the Navy used to need destroyers.

And last but not least from these shores, that zany, long-haired character from rangers, Sunderland and Scotland, who has the name of Jim Baxter, a player who can tune a game to his own composition offering contempt through his long striding runs and shattering passes. 'On you Go', he murmurs to a colleague whom he has supplied with an open prairie to run into.

And to mention finally other half-backs from the world who were instrumental in pioneering new methods, of breaking the half-back free from the shackles of defensive play in which in the old W.M. formation he had to stick on the opposing inside-forward whose job it was to fetch and carry.

Josef Bozsik of Hungary was the 'Erasmus' of that side's 4-2-4 policy, linking up with Hidegkuti in midfield. In this role he was supreme, this parliamentary deputy, conducting the play as if the other side did not exist. And after him came skilled players from Brazil, Zito and Didi, who were as smooth and insidious as panthers.

No. 4s and No. 6s: go on pleasing us.

XV. The Vultures

Two or three thousand people on the terraces at an English Football Combination or Central League match. The 'Stiffs' as they have been nicknamed, or in more polite terms, reserves, kick about their business in an eerie morgue.

They are watched by small groups of staunch supporters, cliques of mysterious men, who drift in off the streets from seemingly nowhere, and shift workers with no more congenial place to go.

A reserve match is seldom a dignified occasion. I used to go to mid-week reserve games in the forties and fifties at Stamford Bridge, White Hart Lane, Griffin Park, Highbury, Loftus Road, Craven Cottage and The Den. Men moved exceedingly slowly on those cold, grey afternoons across the great, empty slabs of terracing. They shuffled to and fro eating peanuts, hanging on crash barriers and howling out their views and grievances. Some spectators preferred to stand on their own against a barrier on the very crest of the terracing, like black, independent shags on a rock, while others massed in a small raucous knot overlooking the halfway line.

These men were often vultures, picking up the bones of the older players who had gone over the top, and were wheezing and struggling against the youngsters. These were merciless men in dirty, torn overcoats, mud-stained brothel creepers and hair drooping over their collars in thick crusts of oil and dandruff. There were sadists, unemployed barrack-room lawyers, and randy labourers on the skive. They were merciless and full of wit, howls of laughter as the home winger went past the balding left-back so that the victim slithered in the mud, his mouth hanging open so that you could see the darkness where his false teeth usually hung.

'Hey, lofty. Put your false teeth back in.'

The visiting centre-half had probably been a noted stopper in the first team, his performances at this ground often proving beyond the means and intelligence of the home team attack. Now he was in the reserves with a paunch, he was a marked man, at least from the terraces. He might be facing a new bustle boy named Bobby Smith, who would soon be going into the Chelsea side at centre-forward and be left dejected on the ground as Smith went past him to shoot aggressively into the top corner of the net.

'GOAL! Get up, big deal!'

The new financial deal for footballers has meant that reserve sides are no longer the graveyards that they used to be. Players are often the off-duty members of the first team squad who regard their outings with the second team as mere convenience to recover their fitness or form. Clubs have also cut down their playing staff. Chelsea in the early fifties, for instance, had fifty professionals and many of these players languished from year to year unwanted in reserve football. And there were always the vultures there to pick your bones.

At Griffin Park, Brentford, there used to be a man who would come along for reserve games with a bazooka on his tongue. Standing there behind one of the goals, he would extract peanuts seemingly from his fly-buttons and attack with lust the performances of a younger player name Jimmy Hill.

Hill, who later had a distinguished career with Fulham, grew a beard, initiated the splicing of the maximum wage, and then went on to Coventry as a manager, was viewed at this time by this man with almost frenzied hatred. Hill had a prominent chin and the man made fun of it as a matter of course. It was unkind but there are some unkind anonymous men along the

Great West Road.

At Chelsea after the war, a crowd of males used to come to barrack Johnnie Galloway, an inside-forward who never quite made it in the first team, but made many appearances with the reserves. Galloway rolled round with a big bottom, an elegant passer of the ball, a frequent marksmen from outside the penalty box, but his trouble was that he didn't look match-fit after war service.

His critics hung over the crash barriers wearing their spiv Trilbys and demob-macs and murdered Galloway in hundreds of words. The merciless baiting would survive the match and go on after Galloway disappeared into the tunnel.

'Go home, Galloway.' 'You bleeder, Galloway. What you playing out there for anyway?' 'God almighty, look at that. The bloke's a fraud.' When Galloway got the odd first team chance, the same band were waiting for him but the larger crowds absorbed their hatred and their vitriol was less obvious, and less hostile.

Going to watch the reserves is like visiting a human zoo. The clank of turnstiles, the silence and emptiness of the terraces, the great stands hanging down over the small, dotted crowd like an aviary and the vultures there are surely vultures huffling, pecking towards another position.

While there, these spectators feel they own the players, that the players are their own property, that they are to be laughed at, scorned at, rejected, discovered, howled at, giggled at, smashed forever onto the scrap heap or found for years of glory in the first team.

The match itself is usually incidental. It is a comic, sometimes savage occasion on which new players come on show and others make football for the very last time.

It is goals which the crowd love. The vultures regarded Bobby Smith as a consoling rampager when he was leading the Chelsea Football Combination side, albeit against ageing defences. At Fulham, the reserve crowds soon learnt to appreciate 'Tosh' Chamberlain as he started thundering down the left wing. Then there was Johnny Haynes, who I saw make his first appearance for Fulham reserves against Queens Park Rangers. The crowd went 'coo' when Haynes scored a penalty which was massively professional for a boy who had only just left school.

Sometimes Haynes and Chamberlain linked up, Haynes offering a benign, schoolboy smirk as his colleague ran the wrong way. When he went the right way he would come thundering towards us and often scored shots which almost tore out the netting.

After these football combination games, if they were on a Saturday, we shuffled up to get the first team result. It if was at Stamford Bridge the news was invariably bad. And a man would grunt 'Two-nought down at half-time. What a hope.'

There would be a long wait while an official got through on the telephone. A long wait, in which the lamplight threw up wavering colours at us in the rain puddles.

'I'll sell my bloody season ticket,' said a man wrapped almost from head to toe in a blue and white scarf. We formed a small lot of people and the feeling in our bellies was of defeat, sure Chelsea defeat, with a team like they had at that particular time they could rarely pull back a two-goal deficit.

The door opened and a man would come out so that you could just see his grey face at the entrance, the warm offices behind him with the calendar of Chelsea Football Club hung up behind the counter.

'Lost 4-0', would be his inevitable words as he banged the door shut.

We would disperse grumbling. 'I'll sell that season ticket, you see,' said the man with the scarf. 'They've got no defence, Bentley's the only bloke here and he 'ain't happy.'

The Fulham Road sucked us up in the midst like a hoover eating cigarette ash and then we would be on our own moving towards the Forum with gloomy thoughts. 'Well, the reserves

won, but who cares about the reserves? Well? Anyhow, why
doesn't Drake give some of the reserves a chance? What's he
up to? He ought to be sacked.'

The crowds at the reserve games at Highbury and White
Hart Lane always seemed bigger, more patriotic, more like the
larger crows who attend Central League and North Eastern
League matches in the Midlands and the North. There was less
of a feeling of music hall entertainment.

There were some fine football combination games at White
Hart Lane during Arthur Rowe's day, and some of his great
push and run side came into the reserves when I was breaking
up. I saw Len Duquemin, the regular first team centre-
forward, play for the stiffs one day and he headed in some
beauties which one could study carefully at close range behind
the net, tons of neck muscle and boom. The crowd called him
'Duckerman'.

'Come on, Duckerman, put another in. Come on the old
man.'

Then there was Tommy Harmer, the perennial, wiggling
weaving creative genius, who was so often lost to Tottenham
reserve football at a time when he could surely have earned an
England Cap. Later he established his place in the Tottenham
side, but it took a long time of lost days in lonely stadiums
playing to a midget audience. On those winter afternoons at
White Hart Lane when he was playing the reserves, his technique stood out in exquisite touches. You could stand near the
corner flag and see him juggling the ball in towards goal from
a short corner, sending a back plunging awkwardly the wrong
way before chipping a perfect cross.

Genius stands out in a reserve match. George Eastham, for
instance, when he was dropped by Arsenal in early 1966 and
out on the transfer list, was reported soon afterwards to have
been prominent, but of course he was prominent. How possibly could Plymouth reserves be expected to stifle his genius.

When Tommy Lawton played for Chelsea reserves against

Arsenal at Highbury in 1947, shortly before he was transferred
to Notts County, a crowd of over twenty thousand came along
to watch him play. If these stars are still in peak condition and
still in possession of their best abilities, they are usually left
alone by the vultures.

It is only when they are over the top that the vultures get at
them and the atmosphere of a local boxing booth is obtained.
Now reserve teams are usually where the younger players are
groomed. The ancients do not clutter up the line-ups so much,
like tombstones marked with numbers. On the other hand, an
older player does stand out much more in a reserve side these
days because of the youthful element.

On a train going up to Norwich I saw Derek Kevan, the
former England and West Bromwich centre-forward reading a
sports magazine. He sat very intently, his head with that famous
lump of wiry hair occasionally swaying to the motion of the
train.

He was now a Crystal Palace player but the young boys
around him with slick groomed pop make ups were not first
team players. Kevan was a member of the Football Combination squad and looking thoroughly out of place. The boys
around him were kids. The head which had blasted in a goal
against the famous Yashin of Russia in Moscow in 1958
seemed out of place. The haircut was nearly a crew-cut but
not quite, the face was losing its youth, slightly harassed, a little
embarrassed. Derek Kevan looked a father among these kids,
but he would not have done so a few years ago when reserve
teams were simply for players who could not get into the First
Division side.

Football clubs have always been anxious to proclaim the
exploits of their reserve sides in first team programmes. It is
perhaps to remind their customers that their reserves do exist.
But only the loyalist supporters read these reports with interest.

In 1948 Chelsea went overboard to push their Football
Combination team which was doing much better than the first

team. The weekly report about the stiffs, or the swifts as the Chelsea reserves have been called, grew more evocative every fortnight. The 'scribe' went to town.

Hence this piece written in the Chelsea programme of 30 October 1948: 'The swifts are in tip-top form, serving up football of character and purpose, have been point gathering at home and away.'

'As an interlude, may we intrude the London Challenge Cup-tie against Crystal Palace, a ding-dong struggle, if ever there was one – it was left until the eleventh hour to receive the well-done, "Pass on Boys."'

'Westward Ho! to the Drake and Raleigh country, "the glories of Devon" took on a new meaning. Two Devon dumplings for two points were good rations for the day. Although the crowds dropped a deluge there was nothing of the "damp squib" about our efforts. Our boys were on top and in no danger throughout.'

'Ken Armstrong sent a ball speeding goalwards which Phil McKnight, who had slipped into a prone position, diverted into the net. Benny Jones, skidding in and keeping his feet, cleverly lobbed the ball over the advancing 'keeper for our second counter.'

'Bob Warren (A Plymothian) was naturally anxious to do his stuff before his "ain" folk, seemed a little excited in the opening minutes but a "whiff" from his native "Ho" have him the "aye steady" to put up a sound display. After the game he was the recipient of warmest congratulations from many of his local friends. Such is sport.'

'Against Queens Park Rangers last Saturday "The Swifts" attracted their largest attendance for two seasons despite the local "Derbys".'

And on Nov 13: 'At Swindon the "Wooden-spoonists" were all stoked up to lower our flag, and starting off at top speed the Railwaymen obviously had no "sleepers" in their team.'

'Running neck and neck, a timely clearance under pressure

found Johnny McKim on the up-line, slipping his guard and veering towards goal, Johnny turned the ball inwards for Hughie Billington to shunt the first, close on half time.

'On the resumption, our boys were forced on the slow line for a period of twenty minutes and our right-of-way was blocked by a checker, but after this breakdown, we got back firmly on the rails again. Nationalising our efforts – a happy band playing full of confidence – to produce our superior craftsmanship, via a defence splitting through ball from Johnny Galloway, for Hughie to "whistle" home our second. From a shuttle service of ground level passes, Ken Suttle got up full steam and tearing past the defences cracked in a terrific shot with terrific force against their "buffer" to rebound to Hughie to drive home the third and his "hat-trick" for the day.'

Such emotional writing may have added a few more spectators to the Stamford Bridge terraces for reserve team games. But they were soon having a go at the players like everyone else. Reserve team matches have always been good therapy sessions.

XVI. Goodison Park: Everton

When Everton came down to London after the war, they were a heavy, declining side and they didn't lay much on. Their meaty, Welsh-international centre-half Tommy Jones, black hair ablaze, jaw solid, eyes flashing, banged the ball downfield and did so again and again; but it usually came back.

Ted Sagar, the former England international who had nested in goal for Everton for over twenty seasons, was still there, but less agile after so many loyal years of service; another pre-war regular Norman Greenhalgh reigned on at left back; Tommy Eglington was on the left wing, a jolly, speedy Irishman with a toothy grin; fat, opportunist Scotsman, Jock Dodds was at centre-forward, banging the ball into the neither he got the opportunity, with the power of a bull going through a thicket.

But Dixie Dean's successor had gone to Chelsea and the side missed Lawton. And Joe Mercer slipped away, not into ageing retirement, but to win honours with Arsenal. They were relegated eventually and came back into the First Division, funnily, second on goal average to Leicester in 1953-54. When John Moores, the millionaire, became chairman, one of the he did was to sack Johnny Carey, a cruel, seemingly harsh act, we thought, and replace him with Harry Catterick, who was handling Sheffield Wednesday.

He had been a player himself with Everton, a tough, resolute, somewhat remote man and he put Everton on top of the League in 1962-63 with a side inspired by a Welshman Roy Vernon, a man with fine control of the ball, and sometimes a temper which flooded in bursts of hot saliva round his lips, and the Scot, Alex Young, a gracious centre-forward.

Everton didn't please everybody, and the supporters they brought with them to Manchester, London and Sheffield, liked to break things in the same way that a child likes to break toys. Everton got their championship but they were nothing like the 1939 side. They faded and the other Merseyside team, Liverpool, took over and the crowds went to Liverpool's Kop. And then in the 1965-66 season were recorded moods of sheer irony.

When Mr. Harry Catterick was knocked on his face outside the Everton coach in Blackpool, early in 1966, it was a surprise and blow to his pride. But fans are fickle, and especially the teenagers, who demand success. His club was down the table and he wasn't playing the stars his supporters were fond of. And yet a few months later Everton won a cup final. What a fickle game it is!

This particular violence stirred from the streets around Goodison Park, where youths, Irish, Scots, Welsh and English, kick footballs against dark Victorian brick walls and play it back again and again and moan about Mr. Catterick while they are doing so.

On a hot summer day in August 1965, I was in a car travelling along Scotland Road with a local journalist. 'They pull these old blocks down and send people to live in new flats but then they want to come back to the dirt,' said the journalist. 'They liked the squalor, they didn't want to leave. It's home. The Beatles moved away. Well, they've got the money. But the ordinary people here, they don't want to leave.'

In the area, people are intensely loyal, but also people liable to go off the rails if they don't get success. They were all round Goodison Park when we pulled up. Kids with footballs, more kids with footballs, more kids with footballs.

In the corner of Goodison Park is a church. A long time ago the club tried to get the church moved to another place and offered to finance the operation themselves. But they never got the church away. It still stands there at the corner of the terracing, as impending and solid as Amiens cathedral. It was there when we arrived, but God seemed miles away, football was right there hanging over the summer streets with the little red, dreary houses and narrow slits for back yards, where darkness covers all.

We were at Goodison to look over their World Cup preparations. At the top of the main stand were the club offices and out of the window was Liverpool, stretching away, old and new grinding together in the heat, brick and reconstruction, and there was no love out there surely, only living and football.

The secretary was noncommittal.

'We are going ahead. You can see when the press will be. We are making arrangements to build a new entrance over there.' He talked in that dry way that some football secretaries have, slightly distrusting us, holding firmly onto his rank and position.

Goodison Park has four stands, high encroaching blocks hanging over the grass but on this day absurdly empty. There was no aggression, no roar of the crowd, far away a women was cleaning the seats slowly and languidly. The seats had human faces and standing looking over at them, rows and rows and rows, one imagined cigars, and hats askew. But the silence was eerie.

Walking behind the infamous goal, where they built a barrier to stop objects crunching into visiting goalkeepers, there was a strange feeling of hostility remaining as if the regulars had never left. The sun blazed down on the pitch which was boiling green, ready for a new season in a few days time. The goals without their nets looked oddly bare like a pair of striptease dancers without net stockings.

How hot it was yet, how cold in the shadow of Park stand. 'I wouldn't stand there on match days,' said the journalist. 'They go mad. There's beer coming out of their navels.'

'All for the sake of a game.'

'No, more than that, the only moment in a week for most of them.'

Behind the park stand, where they were about to reconstruct a new one for £111,400 was a row of Victorian houses. Very typical Victorian houses, small, grubby, red bricked, with outside sanitation. We knocked at one door. A man in shirt sleeves came to the door and looked at us, holding the straps of his braces. His face had deteriorated but his smile brought a gash of youth to a layer of oldish cheese.

He said he and his wife had been found alternative accommodation by Everton, near a cemetery a mile or so away. 'The club has been very nice about it,' he said as his wife ambled out of the shadows in the hall. 'They've found us a handy little place with inside sanitation.'

His wife was plumpish, with glasses shrouding her face. Her apron hung over her breasts like mediaeval armour.

'Bob's lived here for fifty-six years,' he said. 'Saw them all, he did, didn't you Bob?'

'Yes, I've seen 'em all, Dean, Lawton, Mercer, Elisha Scott, Hibbs, Sagar, they've all been in there,' he said waving his thumb towards the rear of the house, where the Park stands loomed over their backyard. 'These houses were built by Everton for their players. You see that house opposite, that was Dean's. Bill lived there. He hated being called Dixie.'

'The crowds aren't the same anymore,' said the wife. 'They have no respect. They come by here and they would break the place up if they could. I'm not sorry to leave. You ought to smell the place on a Saturday. They don't bother to use the toilets.'

'But they are a great team, always were always will be,' said the man. 'You get good football here. Did you see Lawton? Right up that lad, and – boom – down went the ball into the net.'

'He's crazy about football,' said the wife. 'The club have

been good to us. That's a nice house they've got for us by the cemetery.'

We walked along the street in the sunshine and watched boys kicking footballs again. Some of them, the eleven and twelve year olds were going to be great footballers; they could control the ball as easily as chewing a piece of meat. The ones with discipline would go on and make the grade, the others would be lost to football in the cellars of the city, others would become spectators content to stand in the Park. But around Goodison Park that lunchtime, the process of elimination was only beginning. At that moment they were only back alley foot-ballers, all equal.

What was it Joe Mercer said once about back alley foot-ball? 'Back alley football is only a substitute for the real thing. We have to fight for bigger and better playing fields. But all the same it does hold some valuable lessons of its own. For instance, there's this business of playing with a small ball. If you can learn to control a small ball with certainty, you'll find, later on, that the bigger one comes more easily – it's wonderful training for the eye. And the fact of having to play in a confined space or under other difficulties has its advantages.

'The finest outside I ever knew, the best partner I ever had, was one who never spoke a word to me – it was a wall,' said Mercer, who started his career in the back alleys of Ellesmere Port. 'Yes, that wall of mine could always be relied on to return to me the ball when I wanted it – I wish I could say the same for all outside-rights!'

And there around Goodison Park were the new back alley footballers. *Thwack, thwack, thwack* went the ball against brick. 'Pass the pissing thing, wack.'

Harry Catterick wasn't around, or his squad. The stadium hanging above the streets was a giant mausoleum of non-activity. But its very presence controlled all the movements in the streets outside.

'They don't tell better jokes than on Merseyside,' said the

journalist getting into his car. 'You go down to the docks and hear them talk. They've all got nick-names. There aren't four Beatles, you know. There are thousands and thousands of comedians here, too. But football does something for them. They get committed so violently they lose control.'

I thought of that silent, hot day when I read later that Mr Catterick had been knocked down. The boys with the footballs and the empty, cold Park Stand and what could happen when success began temporarily to cool.

XVII. Inside-Forwards

It seems somehow superfluous that Edson Arantes do Nascimento, named Pele, should have to wear a number on his back on the field of play.

But rules are rules, and even Groucho Marx would have to wear a number if he was a player. The number they usually ascribe to the greatest inside-forward in the world is No. 10, but not a soul has to turn to their programmes to see who No. 10 is, because all know Pele. Playing everywhere as he does, from his own goal lines to the very back of the net down the other end, he is unmistakable; a lithe Arabian Night's figure, in the white strip of Santos, or the yellow and blue of Brazil, boots made of sapphires, flesh made of polished mahogany.

So far he has eluded me in the flesh apart from a brief blur seen from a taxi window in Paris as he strolled by with blazered panache staring into the windows of the perfume shops in the Rue de Rivoli.

But there has been television, with a crack-a-jack shots looping into rival nets from incredible distances, runs accompanied by the firecrackers of Brazilian supporters which have taken him past a string of gasping butchers, those moments when the hard realities of the game have been transformed into soccer science-fiction.

To the Brazilians, he is a god and there is no reason to suppose they are wrong. What other player would get bad notices after scoring four goals in a match. The only way to mark Pele, according to professors of the game, is to stand on him relentlessly so close that you are in the position to shave him if so asked or extract a tooth in the legal fashion. Pele has thus taken a lot of punishment in the game and his retaliatory measures have often been somehow justified.

As long as Pele is in the game there is no danger of losing its glamour or mystique. Legions of No. 8's and No. 10's have appeared since the war, of varying rampant talent – Dragoslav Sekularac of Yugoslavia, with a knack of putting the ball through the legs of his opponent, Sandor Kocsis, was *le Tete d'or*, who used his forehead to bang in a stream of goals for Hungary and later Barcelona; Ferenc Puskas of Hungary and later Real Madrid, with a deadly left foot; Gianpiero Boniperti of Juventus and Italy who from 1947 to 1958 played rhythm and blues; Luis Del Sol of Real Madrid, Juventus and Spain, a fanatic for work; Ben Barek, the Moroccan bombshell who played sixteen times for France between 1938 and 1954; Eusebio da Silva of Benfica and Portugal, from Mozambique, with a shot strong enough to leave scars on a custodians fingers; Luis Suarez of Barcelona, Inter Milan and Spain, a link man with the elegance of a cavalry colonel; and that mercurial messiah from Scotland, Denis Law.

These are only a few. Whether fetchers and carriers, linkmen or strikers, they have that natural genius which makes them the *big* money men of a *big* team.

Often these No. 8's and No. 10's can command the highest salaries and drive the finest cars and get up in the morning and have a very cold glass of fruit juice from a refrigerator the size of Notre Dame.

The advantages have not always been so lucid for British No. 8's and No. 10's, who have to play their football in deep Middlesbrough mud and treacly Manchester slime, and live like slaves in conditions far below their potential. But we've had an elegant display – Ivor Allchurch, the Swansea boy, a player of gracious disposition to name just one. And better still, Wilf Mannion, who looked like a choirboy, and spoke his mind about a player's rights. He played for Middlesbrough on a basic salary almost laughable compared with what his output was worth. Old men talk about Stephen Bloomer being the greatest inside-forward of all time, but for later generations, Mannion is the lad.

It was on an afternoon of December midst in late 1950, when White Hart Lane was painted silver like a Whistler nocturne, and the stand roofs stood contentedly on the vapour, that we had ninety minutes of pure Wilf – though less of Eddie Baily whom we came to compare him with.

What a day, what a game. It ended 3-3 with Middlesbrough taking the lead three times against Tottenham, the push-and-run side who were top of the league at the time and moving towards a conquest of that season's championship, and Middlesbrough were second. Lovely stuff, and we came out of the stadium afterwards all cold and damp but licking our chops contentedly.

On that afternoon at White Hart Lane, we saw two inside-forwards in opposition rather than in combination, and if a jury had met after the game to give the verdict on who had won, they would have chosen Mannion, the more complete footballer, who fluttered through the midst that afternoon, his jersey a splash of red blood on the grey scene, holding the centre tunnel of the field with some wiggling runs that sent the Tottenham defence reeling back in confusion.

Eddie Baily, more a puppet to his side's system, and Medley, his left wing partner, was a minor master in comparison.

On a normal day watching Baily's performance would have been a delight, the quick flick to Medley, the dash into the open space for the return with the crowd bellowing him on, but in the mist that afternoon, it was Mannion, lethal and truly in command, who was ruler.

Joe Harvey, the distinguished Newcastle captain and right-half, said once that Mannion made his passes by 'inches' which meant that, he, Harvey, often found himself beaten by inches when he tried to intercept a Mannion pass. Mannion, the blonde and with a strong point of view, which involved him in a number of fracas with his club, was a tremendous worker as well as a stylist. Some say that once bounced off the ball by an offensive defender he would disappear but I never saw this.

Where Baily registered was through his accuracy for finding a man and his acceleration; he also had a natural shot. His part-nership with Medley which went ping, pong, ping, pong, ping, pong, GOAL, was the pepper in Mr. Rowe's scheme and made Baily into an inside-forward feted at All Souls. But out of the push-and-run set up he often seemed ordinary, and lost, when Medley's form began to fade.

After the war we were reared on the Carter and Doherty team, taking them as our ideal pair. There was the Cup Final of 1946 when Stamps scored a hat-trick against Charlton, but it was Carter and Doherty who did the damage. Derby, who came to London early in that first League season since the war, in 1946, brought a move in which Doherty's enormous ability to read the game destroyed Arsenal's hopes.

Leuty, the centre-half, took a free kick and flicked it out to Dally Duncan. The Scottish outside-left zipped away down the wing and flicked it into the centre. Doherty has space to score himself but he distressed the Arsenal defence by flicking the ball instantaneously onto Broome pounding in from the right wing and the balding winger hit the ball into the Arsenal net.

The great inside-forward is able to place himself in the position of taking up the issues of an attack and placing them into lethal perspective, either by changing the pace of the movement, like Ernie Taylor of Blackpool would do, by select-ing a short ball to Matthews, or a long cross-field pass in front of the sprinter Perry, or sending Mortensen away with one of his long runs. In the seconds of passion the decision would be his and his alone.

The basic freedoms of the bold fetchers and carriers, in which they could lie deep, painting the centre circle with

strange, abstract triangles of their own design, are not popular
with managers now, who operate their systems ruthlessly
discarding individualists.

Tommy Harmer, the cultured Jimmy McIlroy and Terry
Venables of Chelsea, have all suffered from this reformation.
An inside-forward now has to score goals and cannot exist on
the luxury of being a crazy ball artist. It was Venables' inability
to fit into Tommy Docherty's rigorous tableaux which led to his
transfer to Tottenham Hotspur.

What will happen to all the future No. 8's and No. 10's?
Will they become evermore numberless in a system when
numbers don't count and a goalkeeper will be expected to play
outside-left as well? Thankfully, that while the inside-forward
artist has been screwed into the new systems, all round players
with the ability to score still exists. Denis Law must be the
inside-forward, because unlike Greaves, who scores triumphant
goals, he also works until his shirt flaps outside his shorts and
he wipes his brow of beads of sweat, walks away with his back
to the goal, but only for a second because there is a sudden
red flash and his scissor kick has put the ball in. He works well
with the explosive Bobby Charlton, less ubiquitous but a calm,
unruffled man with a devastating shot.

Jimmy Greaves remains the enigma. When he started at
Chelsea in 1957 he was a young man with shaven head, long
shorts down to his knees and playing in a side of ifs and buts.
His goal scoring abilities amazed us from the start and goals
were rare then at Chelsea. There was one game I remember
against Preston at Stamford Bridge when he scored a goal from
outside the box still *going* away from the net. But in that flash
moment his left foot had stabbed at the ball in the instant the
last man had been beaten and sent in a shot too fast for Else to
see. Else had to clap.

But while Greaves has scored bucketfulls of these goals
during his subsequent transition from Chelsea to Milan, and
finally to Tottenham, he has not always compensated for his

lack of work in midfield, especially for England. The missing 'fire in the belly' ingredient, which does not linger with English players, is his own, but is has often been his own sickness. Greaves has often looked an ordinary player in the English team, which of course he isn't. What he has to give to our international side may still be sorted away and while his style does not fit into Mr. Ramsey's plans, his use as a danger man is still considerable, his talents compensating for those long, loping disappearances form the scene.

Some of his finest performances were with Bobby Smith in Tottenham, a massive fellow who could take the juice out of an opposing defence while Greaves went through the centre. The inside trio of Greaves, Smith and Haynes in the England side of 1960-61 fared well on this system and in the England-Scotland match of that season at Wembley, Greaves was unstoppable scoring three goals, Smith two and Haynes two, in a record 9-3 victory.

Johnny Haynes who made many a goal for Greaves has seemingly vanished forever from the international scene, one of the hardest workers to wear an England shirt and perhaps one of the most misunderstood. His moods, his bad temper, his ruthless self-criticism made Haynes the first £100 footballer, the subject of hundreds of newspaper headlines. One feels Haynes burnt himself out prematurely toiling for Walter Winterbottom and Tommy Trinder, searching for lost causes.

Toil, toil, toil, and the rewards for these soccer artificers are not as fair as they might be.

XVIII. Talking to Players

Michael Pinner is a goalkeeper. The son of a Boston grocer, he has probably played for more British clubs as an amateur and professional than any other class player since the War. During the week he is a full-time solicitor, on Saturdays flies to Northern Ireland to play for Distillery. He is 31 years of age, lives with his wife and baby and son in a flat overlooking Primrose Hill. The interview took place one evening before he gave a dinner party. As an athlete, he has always been noted for his mania for perfection and tidiness. This comes out characteristically on the field when every ball must be a 'good ball'. It comes out when he is driving, when he verbally blasts any driver who shows the slightest tendency to be sloppy. And it comes out in his own dining room when he sees an orange pip on the floor and attacks it as if he is diving at the feet of an opposing forward.

'I played my first serious game in goal at Boston Grammar School for the under fourteens. But I suppose the time I really became involved was at home when we used to go out into a field with a ball and go kicking around. We used a large, green electricity transformer which was roughly the size of a goal. It was there that I discovered I had the natural attributes for goalkeeping, the ability to hold the ball cleanly, the ability to know where someone was going to kick the ball before he actually did so.'

'Did you play for any teams outside the school?

'Yes, I played for a youth side called Wyberton Rangers

which was run by a man named Al Fox, an experienced player, who turned out for Matlock Town. He knew Eric Houghton, the former England player, who was then the manager of Notts County. He came along to see one of our games.

'With advantages?'

'Certainly. I got a chance with Notts County Reserves in a match at Scunthorpe which we drew 2 – all.'

'Were you frightened?'

'Well, I was anxious. In the first half they crowded me in defence because they didn't trust me. But in the second half, after I had taken a couple of good balls, they gave me space.'

'Did the crowd worry you?'

'No. I have never been worried y the crowd. You don't think about the crowd, you only see the game, it doesn't matter if there are ten, a hundred, or fifty thousand.'

'After school you went up to Cambridge.'

'Yes, and started playing for the university and Pegasus. During the first year in, 1953, I don't think I have ever played better.'

'I remember seeing you play for Cambridge against Bromley. You had an inspired day although your side lost five nil.'

'It was nice having so much to do. That Cambridge side was an extraordinary one. We managed to beat an Arsenal side 4-0 and I don't think we got out of our half more than four times. I really enjoyed my goalkeeping with them.'

'About this time you played your first game for a First Division club as an amateur.'

'It was during the 1953-54 season for Aston Villa against Burnley after Eric Houghton had taken over as manager for Villa. There was a pretty solid hardcore of professionals there like Jackie Sewell, a man who had been around the game, and Frank Moss.'

'Was there a feeling of hostility against a young amateur goal-keeper?'

'No, but I think if I had been a regular player there might

have been.'

'You wanted to be a solicitor primarily rather than a full-time professional goalkeeper?'

'Certainly. This was always my chief concern. After going down from Cambridge, I went to do my articles at Spalding and luckily got a chance playing for Sheffield Wednesday when they were short of a goalkeeper. At the time we were playing in the bottom of the First Division. I played in a few first team games and in the reserves where there were a number of young players who were to be make names for themselves. Kay, Swan and Dobson. It was a wonderful club and the boardroom atmosphere was very good. It gave one the impression of being a big club with solid foundations. The area may have been very depressing but the people living there certainly were not. We won promotion after a spell in the Second Division and then Ron Springett was signed so you might say I was out of work from then on.'

'Well, not entirely. You were by now the England amateur regular choice in which you gained I think fifty-three caps eventually between 1953 and 1965. Wasn't it very confusing playing for so many teams?'

'There was certainly a conflict of loyalties because I was now playing for Pegasus, England and occasionally Sheffield Wednesday. Some of the internationals were rather depressing. My personal best game for England was when we beat Scotland 4-2 at Hampden Park – but it was dismal in that huge bowl with only a scattering of spectators.'

'And then came the Rome Olympics.'

'An extraordinary occasion. The great moment was when we drew 2-2 with Italy when they had a side which included Rivera, the present AC Milan forward. It was a very fast, tremendously physical encounter. I remember the tremendous green of the grass, the greenest I have ever seen, and the floodlights burning down and I felt nervous then. We realized what was at stake. It wasn't an occasion when you say to yourself I am just going out to play. It was something different.'

'After this you had spells as a guest for Arsenal and Chelsea.'

'Only as an emergency reserve. What I remember about Chelsea at that time (1961) was their emphasis on gym work. Training was tremendously hard with emphasis on the stopwatch. It was the first time I had seen the charts of the players' weights and measurements regularly displayed. Arsenal was rather awesome. You felt dominated by the impressive surroundings. There was a feeling of being a big shot although success wasn't in evidence and hadn't been for some time.'

'Then you joined Queens Park Rangers in the Third Division as an amateur. Did you find third division football different from the first?'

'It was more like what one had found in Olympic Games matches. Not as skilled, but hard, although not inherently dirty. In the First Division, footballers tend to stand off. But when they go in, they go in hard. In the Third Division football is less skilled so the defensive player is bound to commit himself more often in the tackle.'

'You were now a full-time solicitor, but national service intervened. Did you play much football in the R.A.F.?'

'I had a season playing for Hendon in the Isthmian League which was disastrous – I found the standard wasn't as high as I would have liked. One found that one was playing in a standard of football where one was expected to do too much, to lead everything. I found I couldn't play in top class amateur football. The pace was too slow and I was anticipating what ought to have happened but did not. I was playing at a different tempo and very badly at that.'

'You turned professional for Leyton Orient in 1963 when they were playing in the First Division. As a class goalkeeper, why hadn't you done so before?'

'Because the financial incentive to turn professional wasn't there. And if I had turned professional earlier, I would have missed those wonderful world tours with the England amateurs.'

'After a time you had a disagreement with Leyton Orient when Dave Sexton became manager?'

'Yes, he wanted me to play full time, but I wouldn't. I didn't want to give up being a solicitor. So I was given a free transfer.'

'And joined Distillery as a part-timer. What is football like in Northern Ireland?'

'Much more relaxed. I no longer want to play at a high point of strain which English top class football requires. At Distillery the atmosphere is Irish. The rat-race is far less apparent.'

'What was your worst game?'

'By that I suppose you mean the game where I let in the most amount of goals. Well, the game I felt most acutely depressed about was in an R.A.F. match against a strong FA eleven, when they hit about ten past me at Peterborough, but there wasn't much I could do about it.'

'How do you feel when a ball beats you?'

'If it's one's fault, one shows it with a gesture of disgust at oneself. Usually I throw the ball back and try and forget about it.'

'While you were at Leyton Orient, you faced the great Spurs championship forward line. Can you say what it was like?'

'You could tell it was a great forward line because they always seemed to have one man over. Jimmy Greaves, for instance, seemed to be merely a member of an attack all of which seemed equally dangerous. One never concentrates on one player. A man is dangerous as the man in front of you who is going to get the ball. When you are playing in goal you don't automatically recognize who is doing the shooting. Very often I have come off the pitch and asked who has scored the goals.'

'What is the most difficult shot that a goalkeeper can have?'

'Definitely the mishit one. This tends to catch you off balance. And then there is the ball which swerves late which is often the case with new balls with shiny surfaces.'

'Can you sum up the exact amount of danger you can

expect when a forward takes a shot?'

'Yes, I can anticipate how difficult a shot is going to be sometimes by the speed in which a man takes a shot. The speed with which the ball travels through the air is not so important.'

'Has goalkeeping changed since you came into the game?'

'Only in distribution. It used to be regarded as the last line of defense, now we regard it as the first line of attack. When I first started, goalkeepers rarely threw the ball. Frankly I can't see any further development for a goalkeeper now.'

'What about training? Do you like it?'

'The only training I really like is practicing with the ball, short sprints and agility work. I don't find there is any purpose served in long runs.'

'How did you find the professional game as compared with the amateur?'

'Professionals don't seem to be any different from any other working man. They have a drink after the game and then go home. Amateurs tend to bitch more about other colleague's faults. I found after professional games that professionals don't boil over if another player has played badly. I think the professionals realize that if a player has reached a certain ability they can be excused their off days. Amateurs niggle, they always tend to mention a bad performance.'

'What is your opinion of a good manager?'

'One who has the respect of his players, has a knowledge of football which is always evident and an ability to lead his team. There is a good deal of dimness in the game on the management side, lack of ability to translate ideas into practice.'

'Who is your ideal goalkeeper?'

'Grosics, the Hungarian... because of his agility. It was fantastic how long he went on. He had complete command.'

'Why do you think you are physically attuned to be a goalkeeper?'

'I think I have an ideal build which is not too heavy, like Peter Bonetti of Chelsea and Bill Brown of Spurs, and I have long fingers.'

'Do you daydream much during a game?'

'I always concentrate upon the game. There isn't time to think of anything else.'

'When do you begin to feel anxious?'

'The moment of trouble comes when you see that the other side are coming through with one man over. Then you must think that in about three moves time you are going to be in trouble.'

* * *

Archie Andrews is the licensee of the Britannia public house, in Clarendon Road, W.8. He retied from playing football as a left-half, chiefly in the Third Division, three years ago. He is a quiet, almost classic example of the old-time pro, with his black hair parted down the centre. He keeps a scrapbook in his pub which is filled with cuttings about third Division football in the fifties, when he played for Crystal Palace and Queens Park Rangers. One night we talked about his career and how he felt about the game.

'Where did you play your first football?'

'At Alton Secondary Modern School in Hampshire – Jimmy Dickinson was there as well but was older than me and I never played in the school team with him. Playing the game came naturally, Eddie Lever, who was later full-time manager at Ports-mouth was my teacher. He used to say I turned very quickly on the ball. From School I went into the local town side, Alton, at the age of sixteen.

'I signed amateur forms for Tottenham in 1947 but then didn't hear anything more from them so I signed for Ports-mouth as a pro. I was in the reserves during their championship year 1948/49 but didn't get into the first team because Jimmy Dickinson was so consistent. I was on £12 a week at Portsmouth, good pay. They were a good club because they were on top. I think they were so good because they were experienced, an elderly side but fit, and fast. After the army, in which I formed the Royal Corps of Signals half-back line with my two brothers – a proud moment – I moved to Crystal Palace for a transfer fee of £2,500. They were in the Third Division at that time in 1950.

'It was hard football, made harder because we were struggling. When Laurie Scott was manager he wanted us to play football; when Cyril Spiers took his place, he cut that idea out. In the Third Division we were not allowed to play football. You have to play tighter because you are crowded all the time. It's hard rather than tough. I found Crystal Palace was where I played my best football. I was an attacking wing-half. I used to hit anything that came at me. I used to crack in goals anywhere from forty yards.

'I moved to Queens Park Rangers in 1957 and played for them for three seasons and found them a little fair club, but we didn't have much of a policy. Jack Taylor, the manager, was a typical Yorkshireman. We used to have tactical talks. They didn't really work out. There was one move that Taylor was keen about with an inside-forward acting as a thrown-in decoy, which had worked when he was a player at Sunderland, but it never worked with us although he made us do it hundreds of times. Spiers also had tactical talks at the Palace which lasted for three or four hours sometimes, but if you asked any questions afterwards you wouldn't be playing next week. He had his set ideas. He wanted plenty of big boot, plenty of crunch.'

'Didn't you mark Len Shackleton in a cup tie?'

'Yes, that was a laugh, Jack Taylor told me to go all out and if I couldn't stop him, kick him. I went out on the park and I didn't get near him until the second half. We fell down after my tackle and he got up and said "Shall we dance?" He was the best inside-forward I've played against. He was so cheeky with the ball, the sort of player if you wanted to play the game straight he wouldn't be associated with you.

'I moved into Southern League soccer with Sittingbourne. I could have gone to Watford but I had no intention of staying in the game. I wanted to do something else – like having a pub of my own. I'm quite happy now.

'Sittingbourne was a first class club run by Wally Rickett, the former Blackpool player. When I was there we won everything and the pay was good.'

'What was the life like as a professional member of a Third Division club in the fifties? Was there much discipline?'

'Well, there were some pretty daft ideas. At Palace we had a little hide-away under the stand so we could have a quick fag during our lapping sessions. Once when we went out onto the Park for a session, when it was covered in snow, our trainer went off round the pitch and came back and said, "It's no good running round that way, but if you run round the other way, you'll be all right."'

'And the discipline?'

'Most clubs give you a book when you arrive which says you must be inside your home by 10.30 and things like dancing are out after Wednesday. Otherwise what you did like sex and drink was left to your own discretion. Quite a lot of things went on at away games, I can tell you.

'I always had a couple of pints of bitter or Guinness before a game, something to sweat out. But I always trained seriously. I thrived on roadwork rather than lapping round the track. Lapping is a drag.' .

'Basically I took it as a living. I took it in my stride. I never found there was much bad feeling among the players. You don't often find players squaring up to one another. But you get a lot of players who run to the manager. They're the ones who are the first out of the bath. Players are temperamental. The difference between the ordinary ones and the brilliant ones is that the brilliant ones are thinking all the time. If you had eleven players thinking every game, that side would win everything. You can say that during a game at least two players of a side will be playing below standard each week. As for managers, I've generally found them to be "yes-men".

'I don't like the new methods myself. We taught the rest of the world to play the game and now we are letting them dictate the game themselves. The way to beat these foreign sides is to have two wingers who are capable of beating the full-back and cracking in goals like Harris and Froggatt did at Portsmouth. A side in possession will always dictate the play.'

* * *

Jimmy Greaves calls soccer 'the business'. One day after training at Tottenham we had a chat about his business after nearly ten years as a working member.

'How do you feel the game has changed since your first league game for Chelsea?'

'When I first came into the game, there wasn't much thought behind it. In the old days it was all the long ball through the middle. But now there has been a revolution. Obviously one has to adapt oneself to new ideas.

'Now you have to work in a much tighter situation. Football is somewhat defensive these days. You can't get a ball through as you used to be able to. Therefore you have got to look for a wall-passing type of game, running onto a ball laid sideways.

'I have often been asked why I haven't scored five goals in a game since I came to Tottenham. Defenders have got far more intelligent these days. You do well to keep up a players' standard as a forward, if you average thirty goals you are doing very well.

'I probably enjoy the game more, there are less worries. I have got six, maybe eight years to iron out now. It worries me if I don't score during a game. I get concerned about scoring, but this unfortunately is what people expect me to do.

'It's a bit unfortunate I have got this role, so I hope to score every game I play. I get a lot of satisfaction by playing well, but I prefer to score because it keeps the spectators happy.'

'You don't seem to work into Mr Ramsey's ideas about his 4-3-3 World Cup system?'

'Well, from what I can see systems like these go by the board at Wembley. The pitch isn't designed for any systems. It is a big pitch, a true pitch. It boils down to how well England play. There is nothing new in the 4-3-3 system which I haven't done already.

'Let's face it, whatever system you play, the better team will win. We are only on the fringe of defensive-play football over here I experienced the real thing while with Milan. If you won 2-1 there, it was considered good going.'

'What is your average week like?'

'On Mondays I'm off and devote most of my time to the packaging business I run at Romford. I'm out and about with my brother-in-law getting customers, travelling up north and that sort of thing.

'We have got young kids so I'm up at 6.30. I have a good breakfast and then leave for business (training) at 9.15 on Tuesdays to Fridays. On match days I have a lay-in until eight o'clock and if I am in a hotel, sleep until ten. In that case I don't eat anything until the pre-match meal. I haven't got a big appetite but I eat well. I like taking the wife out to dinner, Chinese, Italian food, Indian curry and I also like pub restaurants.'

'Do you like entertainment outside the game?'

'Well I watch television all the time. I'm easily pleased. I like going to the cinema to see spy films, any old ones.'

'Do you consider yourself a business man?'

'Well, you might say my two executive touches are my modern, detached house and Ford Zodiac. But most professional footballers don't lead the sort of film-star, glamour life that many people believe. We are working-class players and come from working-class backgrounds.'

XIX. Wingers

We in England live in a dull, wingless era in which Mr Alf Ramsey plays inside-forwards in No. 7 and 11 shirts with a roving commission which can spread deep into their own penalty areas. Chelsea, too have an inside-forward operating on their left wing, and a centre-forward on the right. It is necessary but boring.

Stanley Matthews, the Rembrandt of Soccer, disappeared last year and his retirement brought to an end the last vestiges of majestic dalliance by gifted egoists, a kingdom he ruled and inspired on the patch of grass stretching from the half-way line down the right flank of the pitch to the corners of the penalty box which creep out into the field like the select fringes of a garden square.

The Matthews dalliance, the shuffling, itchy, twitchy, wiggle, the sudden acceleration outside the full-back, the burst and pass before two defenders could reach him, the devastating centre curling in from the wing, or the short ground pass after beating the back, pulled back just out of reach of the goalkeeper, will never be seen again.

We live in a time when the cupboard is bare of class wingers; Peter Thompson, of Liverpool, yes, but not quite: something is missing; Cliff Jones, of Spurs and Wales, yes, a lovely manner and superb in the air; George Best of Manchester United and Ireland, a Beatle-haired, insidious mover with a flair for fast cars, yes, a seemly splashy colourful dresser who is probably the best we have in the country right now.

But there was a time after the war when wingers lined up in far more profusion, independent and devastating as a select band of archers.

There was Tom Finney, who after the war amazingly kept Stanley Matthews out of the team for a number of matches, and of whom the *Sunday Dispatch* critic wrote, of his debut against Ireland in 1946: 'Few players in the history of football have had such a triumphal international debut as Finney, who toyed with his opponents, scored one goal, and made two more. (His) footwork and body swerve made Ahearne look a Shire horse…'

Ahearne suffered and so did hundreds of class full-backs and there was worse to come when Finney switched to the left flank and Matthews came in on the other flank.

The Portuguese melted away, with tears in their eyes, when these two got down to nibbling their flanks in the spring of 1947 and from nibbling, bit, and bit hard, until the small-sized ball with the assistance of Lawton, Mortensen and Mannion hit their net ten times.

Finney may have murdered many class full-backs, but he always approached the task of beating his opponent as a special type of jingle to cut a path through, full of various cunning thickets that might hold him and demon spikes growing from every blade of grass to stop his progress.

As he recognized, and said, very few class full-backs were 'slow-witted', and each one had to be valued on a high level, but their faults he certainly found and exposed so that he left them sitting on the park chewing gum and looking dumbfounded.

Speed off the mark, an exceptional ability to centre at speed, masterful ball control and a gift of giving a full-back a series of confidence tricks by never really suggesting that he was full out during a burst and then increasing the burst to double its speed were all in the Finney make up.

With his curly hair, a thin smile cutting across his face like the grin of a bounding hare, his calm, unruffled demeanour, he was a plumber playing football and playing football as well as anyone else has ever done, a great player who later switched to centre-forward and scored goals by making use of his dribbles through the middle, and slipping the ball past a goalkeeper as if he was posting a letter.

Sometimes his faults could reduce us to gnashing rage, the obvious fault of over-dribbling, an obvious tendency of an artist with a love of the ball. If he had been a painter he would have scrubbed these particular canvasses but in football the performance and the fault is only momentary and faults cannot be rectified. He would have scrubbed the F.A. Cup Final of 1954 canvas against West Bromwich when he had a dull day, when dullness was the last thing called for.

Matthews had two bitter days at Wembley, in 1948 and 1951, but he finished up on the winning side in 1953 with a performance which Finney must have longed to repeat but couldn't, against a reasonable but not sensational West Bromwich side. Matthews who has been dealt with in abundance elsewhere, is one's winger in a lifetime and there cannot be anyone to replace him with a league career which started the year I was born and finished on a misty day in 1964 at the Victoria Ground, Stoke, against Fulham, and a masterful performance it was.

Stanley came down to the hotel before the game to meet the Fulham players and everyone treated him like a retiring professor, respectfully, with a touch of humour. It seemed to bring out the extravert in Johnny Haynes who smiled broadly as Stanley shook hands and walked around with his neat suit, a natty tie, a quiet, gentle person in a room of youthful players.

Stanley, the Wizard of Dribble, the Old Master, his hair glued back over his head, came out of the pallid, smoky, bricked blur of the potteries, and gave us thirty years of genius, spanning games and games and games that cannot be forgotten and the men who helped him acknowledge this with wonder and admiration, Raich Carter, Ernie Taylor, Wilf Mannion, Stanley Mortensen and others.

Once sitting on the touchline at White Hart Lane, where the photographers were, I could have touched him as he wiggled up the by-line. Those hands held out slightly, the shuffle, the spurt and then there was the heaving and straining and pushing and shouting as the Spurs defence jostled up to put the ball away and stop Mortensen and Perry from the coup de grace. And Stanley always going through on the outside, and coming again, and Withers in trouble again, not knowing whether to go forward, not knowing whether to take the bloke and make a fool of himself again, or hang back, and others tried to help him but Stanley was too fast for them going onto meandering runs into midfield, spreading out the passes with delicate prods across the mud, and when he was near the goal we could hear the delicate slap, slap of his boots on the ground which you never hear from the terraces because of the noise. 'Bloody marvelous,' said the photographer. 'How old is the bloke now? Sixty?'

Then there are other wingers but they are in another gallery, a lesser school for minor masters, the difference between Rembrandt and Reynolds.

But consider minor masters all the same, Hanocks and Mullen at Wolverhampton, who ate up the turf and shot like centre-forwards after cutting in; Bobby Mitchell, of Newcastle, who floated past full backs and went round them again just for luck, Billy Liddell of Liverpool with a ferocious shot Frank Blunstone of Chelsea, a courageous player, who came back after twice breaking a leg, and gave his club loyal service, despite running into numerous cul-de-sacs; Charlie Mitten, of Manchester United, a nasty winger to have lurking in your penalty area, Bobby Langton, of Bolton and Preston, speedy and powerful, Willy Waddell of Rangers, who never graced English football but put fear in our stomachs at Wembley internationals; and another Scot, Gordon Smith, both of whom were in the Alec Jackson tradition. And Medley of Spurs push-and-run side playing duets with Eddie Baily; Harris and

Froggatt of Portsmouth, rare smackers of the ball, they come to mind every time one looks at the four corners of White Hart Lane, Highbury and Stamford Bridge, where they did things in motion which were delicious. They were wingmen who played with something extra penal, which did not amount to running forward like Los Angeles speed cops; they were dangerous each in his own particular way, but such delicious power and persuasion could rarely be dulled or dimmed by ruthless tackling because of being real professionals, they took a crunch and came back for more.

And the foreigners, of course, with Garrincha, the Bird, the foreigner on the wing, so fast in bursts that his blue and yellow Brazilian strip flashed like a strange 'bird' of paradise winging through a dark forest; and Gento of Real Madrid who, flat out, was a sprinter who could not be caught; and Hamerin of Sweden, a cut-throat when in possession of the ball, and the tank-like Rahn of West Germany, who sped up and down the wings during the 1958 World Cup with Bavarian hunting horns blasting him on.

To watch pretty things being done by a winger is one of the chief pleasures in watching football; to see a back beaten by sheer individual buffoonery and then see the winger cut in on goal with a clear path to either make a shot or cross the ball for a centre-forward to nod in, is a moment when the other side has been fooled by grandeur.

This is not the age of the egoist on the wing, it is not allowed by the compact make up of 4-2-4 or 4-3-3. Often the full-backs are more involved with running up the flanks than the wing men themselves, pulled back into the deep and lost in a maze of managerial tactics. Yes, a pity but necessary in this era of defensive football. But the age of Matthews and Finney, who followed other great egoists, like Billy Meredith, Alec Jackson, and Alan Morton, will never be forgotten. Those years when we said: 'Look out, the old man's got the ball.'

XX. Goalkeepers, the Barmy Lot

When I lived in Chelsea, the flower seller on the other side of the square was the father-in-law of a famous international goalkeeper of the period. The 'keeper was good enough to have played for England for some time but his vulnerability was from shots fired from outside the box.

Some strange nervous ailment assailed him at the sight of the white ball spinning in from great distances and with constant regularity the ball would float past his despairing dive and finish in the net. It made a nice picture for the photographers but for the victim it was cruel.

His father-in-law defended these lapses on many misty mornings as he sold his dusty chrysanthemums to the randy, leather-encased wives of city men.

'It was the wall,' he said. 'They blocked his vision' or 'Those floodlights. He hadn't a chance.' Or 'it caught so an so's boot and went in off the centre-half.'

The flower seller had his views but we knew secretly that this goalkeeper had a fault and that these were excuses. Meanwhile his prowess in stopping the ball fired in from five yards from an elephantine centre-forward remained. But nothing could stop him from being a bad goalkeeper in dealing with high balls.

He was keeping goal at a time when the standard of goalkeepers in Britain had declined. People mourned the loss of Frank Swift, Jimmy Cowan, Ted Ditchburn, Bert Williams and others, good enough to play for their countries, who hadn't been allowed to because the standard was so high. The War period produced some exceptional goalkeepers. One of my first joys from football was seeing a photograph in *Picture Post* of Tiger Khomich, the Dynamo goalkeeper who played on the 1945 tour of Britain. Crouched over the ball in all black, he looked like a gorilla with a stomach ache, but when he took off accelerating full stretch across the turf his whole body doubled in size.

The great god of post-war goalkeeping – Frank Swift – was killed in the Munich air disaster while travelling as a journalist. Unfortunately I never saw Frank play a really good game. In those league games for Manchester City he seemed almost aimless as if retirement was near at hand, as it was. And in the England–Scotland international of 1949 at Wembley, when Houliston charged into him and injured a rib, he naturally looked jaded. But even before his injury, his dive to reach a shot from Mason which beat him was the action of a man who is at an end.

But Swift was the mystique, the big man who dominated his area, picked up the ball one handed, with a huge paw, looked at the lace and threw it to one of his backs. This was his invention and it made the backs take up positions which made them work twice as hard and doubled their effectiveness.

Swift, the England captain in Turin against Italy in 1948, making a number of unbelievable springs; Swift, hurling himself across the goalmouth against Wales in 1946 and catching the ball as easily as if it was a child's woolen ball; Swift, towering above the opposing forwards in his yellow international jersey, an old rustic cap pulled down on his ears. Swifty was the king.

The strength of British goalkeeping them was consistency. Our goalkeepers now with their flashy all green strips and ski caps may look more proficient and acrobatic in the Contintental way, but you often see them make elementary mistakes. It was during this period after the war that goalkeepers like George Swindin, (Arsenal), Ditchburn (Spurs), Jack Sanders

(West Bromwich) and Gilbert Merrick (Birmingham) could rarely be faulted week after week. When they plodded out into a stadium towards their nets, flinging their caps into a clump of grass you felt that the shots which beat them would have to be good ones. They hated being beaten.

Ditchburn was a tremendous acrobat, who could do wonders with a high ball fired into the top corner, Swindin was solid and undemonstrative, who loved the low ones fired in from Mullen of Wolves or Hurst of Charlton along the ground. There was that great save he made against Wolves at Highbury in 1946, it came in low and burnt his fingers but he got there. Jack Sanders, West Bromwich, an elegant, careful goalkeeper and the orderly, unspectacular moustached Merrick, whom the Hungarians shattered later.

Then there was Sam Bartram who floated in the air and bounced right out of his goal and kicked clear with the joy of a man kicking a rubber ball in the surf. Sam never played for England, although he might have done, but for Swift. But there were instances when he lost his concentration and let in the simple ones.

The two goalkeeping performances I can't get over were both in 1949. The first was at Wembley in the England-Scotland match when Scotland had a goalkeeper nobody south of the Border had ever heard of called Jimmy Cowan. They had all heard of Swifty, at the other end, but that wasn't his day.

Cowan, in his yellow jersey was a piece of elastic that afternoon against Mortensen, Pearson, Milburn, Finney and Matthews. The shots that poured towards him in those opening twenty minutes were all good ones usually going away from him, particularly one searing effort from Milburn, but the yellow flash took off and reached and held them all.

Wembley was stunned, but not the Scottish side, who took over from Cowan's inspiration and won well by 3-1. Cowan on that day was unbeatable. He had one of those days when everything was his and the goal that did go in from Milburn was a mere deflection.

Cowan hardly needed a defense in front of him that day. In the early minutes this defense was overrun anyway and Cowan was often left on his own. When you had a player like Stanley Mortensen flying down on you alone and unchecked the prospects for a goalkeeper were pale. Mortensen moved like a dragon fly darting over still water, a ripple of white and black movement and then a blur as he let fly from the edge of the box.

Cowan at Wembley on that sunny afternoon had to stand up to a number of these moments, but when the ball came in he was there flinging his body towards the scoreboard, seizing the ball on the line.

The other spectacular was at White Hart Lane, on a cold, misty winter afternoon later that year, when England were made to look very stupid indeed by the Italians. It was the handsome blond Bert Williams – 'The Cat' of Wolverhampton Wanderers – who saved our lumbering side as the Italians tiptoed past Franklin, Ramsey, Wright, and the rest like phantoms drifting through a solid forest. But Williams was always there to palm the ball away, to hurl his athletic body in all directions so you could almost hear the torso shout: 'No more, no more, I can't stand it.'

Again and again Williams plunged to cut out balls from Boniperti and Carapallese; on one occasion as we split down the terraces in that 70,000 crowd behind the goal, Williams managed to divert the ball with his legs as he was diving in opposite directions... 'Ooh, ooAH!' roared the crowd, and the Italians held their heads in frustration. The Italians never beat Williams that afternoon and England nipped in two late goals to win the game, Williams' game.

A goalkeeper of the moment who reminds me of the Bert Williams mould, is Peter Bonetti of Chelsea. He is spectacular in the way Williams was with a phenomenal leap and split-second anticipation. He has the same knack of being able to turn back at the last second to deal with a deflected ball or one of those nasty daisy-cutters which come whipping up out of the floodlights.

Bonetti has improved enormously since the last year or two, in keeping with his sides gorgeous rise. He is a self-critical lad who is always ready to admit his mistakes. There was a time when these were far too frequent and I remember one match against Walsall, when Chelsea were chasing promotion, when he made a poor clearance to an opposing forward who simply lobbed the ball over his head into the goal. Those days seem to have gone.

His performance against Leeds in a recent Fourth Round Cup tie was a classic. He literally did not make a mistake and during the dying seconds, when Jack Charlton smashed in a certain goal, he somehow fell on the ball and held it with the stadium wailing.

He will surely go a long way and must be a rival to the more solid, efficient, almost old-fashioned Gordon Banks of Leicester who wears our yellow jersey.

Before the Hungarian 'revolution', our goalkeepers wore heavy green woolen jerseys, long shorts, thick shin pads and greasy caps. George Swindin shattered the Highbury crowd in 1948 when he appeared wearing a white ski cap for a match against Manchester United. He was soon back wearing the greasy cap. The crowds didn't like a player looking different... I wonder what they would have felt about Bonetti's all green strip and green skiing cap. Booed him, perhaps, for being a reactionary.

Victor Woodley, Chelsea's great international goal-keeper before the war, was never without his greasy cap. He wore it with the regularity of a farmer and it was on his head when he kept goal for Derby in the 1946 Cup Final.

Victor was a pre-war goalkeeper; by the end of the war his re-flexes weren't as quick and he often couldn't reach the low ones and he often couldn't reach the high ones; and he fumbled crosses.

When he played against Chelsea in 1947, it was one of his last games for Derby before going to Bath City.

Tommy Lawton beat him with a snapshot from outside the box and Victor went down to it slowly and it was five years past him before he hit the ground. There was an almost apologetic grin on his face as he picked the ball out of the net, because he would have saved that shot for Chelsea ten years before, and one felt he didn't want the crowd to see him in decline.

Goalkeepers can be very funny. Swift himself said there was something 'crazy' about being a goalkeeper. But if they are crazy, they are unique, and if they are injured during a game and someone else takes over, the difference is vivid.

I once saw Johnny Carey take over from Crompton in the Manchester United goal and he did some very odd things, like punting the ball in the wrong direction and fisting the ball twice and then heading it away with that shining bald head. He didn't let his side down that day but he didn't look a goalkeeper.

A goalkeeper is a man on his own based in an open box with a net and alone with his problems. Some walk up and down their eight feet cages looking down at the ground; others stand with their arms folded; some stand on the edge of the penalty box shaking with frustration; others talk to photographers. Some, like Tony Macedo of Fulham, harry their defense and continually shout at them; others look remote and unconcerned, or stylish and safe. Some, like Sam Bartam, like to bound out at the slightest provocation, and kick the ball away from an opposing forward coming through but not quite in control.

Bartram did this once but only kicked the ball against the on-coming forward's shins and Bartram found himself running back behind the forward who had only to tap the ball into the net. Sam must have said something rude because the forward shot the ball yards wide.

Goalkeepers have their own particular tricks and ploys

to stop a raiding forward, out on his own, the wind flowing through his hair, a slight sneer on his face.

After dribbling round his rival and smiling effusively while raining a boot to clout the ball into the net, the forwards find himself seized around the crutch. The forward caught by this bear-like rugby tackle, lets out a flow of abuse before disintegrating into the mud.

A goalkeeper in defeat is as sad as a stray dog searching for his kennel or a man snubbed by a woman half his age. They hover alone in the corner of the dressing room pulling off their mud-caked jerseys, their jaws sunk towards their chests, a look of total recall on their faces. They are figures alone, holding responsible the whole disaster of the afternoon on their shoulders.

After the 1956 F.A. Amateur Cup semi-final, between Hendon and Finchley at Highbury, I went down into the dressing rooms. There were a lot of hangers on and officials in the Finchley dressing room, and a big Hendon director rather sheepishly offering champagne to the losers. 'Well done, bad luck lads. You'll be there next year.'

Johnny Adamson, the goalkeeper, was first in the bath rubbing soap round his pubic hairs and not saying anything. 'Bad luck Johnny,' I said. 'You had a good one'. 'Thanks, but so did Hyde,' he said shrugging. 'Can't he shoot?' Johnny wasn't moping but he was disappointed. He had made one incredible save in the top corner with a frame which was by no means light. But he couldn't stop the Hendon goals and he thought of each one as he gout out of one of those marble baths which make Highbury into the Ritz of the football business, water running down his legs. Sadly he dried himself and sat down on a bench. It isn't nice to be knocked out of the semi-final.

Goalkeepers are the most human of people. They all make mistakes, even Yashin, the 'octopus' of Russia, and Grosics, that lithe, prancing panther of Hungary. But the good ones remain good if they keep their consistency and these two can rarely be faulted over the years.

Two goalkeepers that I would personally like to have, if I had a league team, would be Jack Kelsey of Arsenal or Bert Trautmann of Manchester City. Kelsey, the strong, well-built Welshman, and Trautmann, the former German paratrooper who broke his neck during the 1956 Cup Final, combined all the attributes of a class goalkeeper – safety, anticipation, distribution, acrobatics, enormous reach and control of the area. These men were goalkeepers.

XXI. Griffin Park: Brentford

When Brentford played Bristol Rovers, in a Third Division match at Griffin Park one damp, gusty day in February 1966, I was sitting behind a man with a small, thin moustache hunched up in a fading cavalry twill overcoat. He was a season-ticket holder.

Brentford were at the bottom of the Third Division. He offered no hint of comfort or loyalty to the sweating struggling side throughout the seventy minutes he watched the game before shambling out of the stadium to be swallowed up in the 'valve, tube and fittings' desert of the Great West Road. During the game I made a note of his remarks.

Brentford played badly that day. Bristol Rovers split their defense apart as easily as shelling a pea pod, with Biggs, a gargantuan centre-forward, scoring three goals which went past Chick Brodie like bullets. The final score was 0-5 a score which led to a hostile demonstration outside the Brentford offices after the game, but the man with the square moustache had left long before then.

He had sat down on his hard, wooden seat two minutes after the kick off, watching the game with his left shoulder pointing to the stand on the opposite side of the field. Crossing his legs and occasionally scratching a waxy ear, he watched Brentford make a number of futile attacks on the Rovers goal like a weasel waiting to nip a rabbit's neck. Then the barracking began:

'Come on, idiot, get it right, the goal is the other end, twat, fool, this is football…

'You big, gangling fool…

'Beautiful pass to Bristol that, terrible innit terrible. Aren't they paid to play this game?

'Well done, pass it to Bristol…

'Oh, a good pass for once…

'Come on you idiot, come on Block…

'Crikey, wake up, clot. Come on, get into him, you idiot, fool, you stupid fool, wake up you lot.'

An old man with a severed jaw turned round and whispered: 'Why can't you show some loyalty to the Bees?' he looked pained. And his friend, a fat man with an R.A.F. tie said 'You're having a go, aren't you?'

Brentford missed an open goal. 'I am so fed up with it. I've got money in this Club. I'm so fed up with it.'

'Well done, pass it to Bristol…

'They're bottom, do you know that? Do you know why I go on so? I go on because you can't get excited watching it so you must excite other people. Come on the bottom Club…

'WAKE UP, you wingers, move there you idiot, you twit…

'WAKE UP Block. Don't you know when you're offside?'

'YOU HEAP OF RUBBISH. WAKE UP BLOCK, you idiot. Look, some of them are going already…'

· Behind the net of Bristol Rovers, a couple wearing crash helmets were no longer watching the game. They were embracing tenderly, their crash helmets touching like two golf balls.

'To think I used to sit here and watch Brentford in the First Division. WAKE UP YOU DEFENDERS' (Rovers missed a chance) – 'It would be nice if we missed one or two…'

'Pass it to Bristol, you rotten lot…

Bristol Rovers scored their first goal, Jones moving square across the pitch to send Jarman through with an exquisite pass and Biggs pounding in made Brodie's heart give a berserk twitch.

'Well done, good goal, goal goal. They've got you, you twits.'

Fifty seconds later Biggs hurtled through on his own and scored with a shot of such power that the ball rebounded back towards the centre circle. 'Well done, a good goal, you see what they're doing to you, you gormless twits…'

After half-time he sat farther away from the old man with the severed jaw. Perhaps he did not want to offend him any more, perhaps he felt disturbed by this loyal man who never once uttered a squeak of criticism as his team was reduced from hopeful plodding to sheer mediocrity.

When Mel Scott, the old Chelsea centre-half, and one of the few players having a reasonable game for Brentford, rose up to head a goal of enormous violence against his own side, I waited for the man with the moustache to make further comments. But none came. He had visibly paled, his moustache twitched as if moved by the popping bogs of hell.

He was speechless and then suddenly, as play re-commenced, his voice rose in hoarse whisper: 'Brentford, I don't love you any more. I don't love you, you gormless twits…'

'Why don't they buy George Eastham' shouted a voice down in the Enclosure.

'What, for a farthing?'

The barracker missed the last two Rovers goals, slipping out silently in the rain, looking for verbal support as he made for the gangway. But none came.

The old man with the severed chin watched him with deep hatred.

'What we need is some loyalty around here. It was loyalty which took us up from the Third Division to the First in the Thirties. What kind of club can this be, with types like that?'

XXII. The Crowd

'The crowd are as much as part of the atmosphere
as the air, the rain, the sun and the midst…'
BERNARD JOY

There is always the match and there is always the crowd. Without the crowd it wouldn't be the same match because, with a yelling, baying, bawling crowd around him, a player's metabolism rises as each swell of sound gushes towards him from the terraces as he heads for goal. If there was no crowd he would still be heading for goal, but there would be no sound to make him wallow in the moment, in which needles of piercing devotion are driven into his blood stream from the terraces, uplifting his efforts.

And those who make it so are the supporters clustering in heaps of red and blue and white and black and yellow behind the goals on the kop, in the West Stand, in the East Stand, at the peak of the terraces, down on the sidelines, supporters swathed in colour with loud, raucous voices and long, lingering tongues and Liverpool choruses up their sleeves ready like 'Eee, Aye Adio, we're off to see the Queen.'

Those supporters who make the rat-a-tat-tat sound on the terraces – '*Everton-da-da-da – Everton*' '*Chel-Sea – Chel-Sea – Chel-Sea*', or let their voices roll into 'Glory, Glory Hallelujah, The Spurs go Marching On' or down from Newcastle, 'Seeing the Blaydon Races' or those famous Pompey chimes one used to hear in the late forties 'Deum Pompey Pompey Deum', are the ulcerated hard core with whom an ordinary, shy spectator feels no real bond or brotherhood, only a condescending admiration from afar.

It is the people with the sound who make the long journeys round the country, nestling into second-class carriages of excursion trains at dawn to flow into a strange foreign landscape where their ultimate aim, terraces of their host's stadium, greet their eager eyes early in the afternoon and over which they scramble waving rattles and muttering gentle obscenities after a beer or two.

The match result makes their week and if they lose, particularly Merseysiders, a grim cloud of depression falls on them and some, will even go so far as to rip out a train toilet pan and fling it onto the track as a parting message of contempt for a departing town.

The trains they travel on take the brunt of their frustration, being burnt and beaten, and peed and spat on, because a referee disallowed one of their side's goals, and as for the railway seats they make lovely, soft objects to slice up with a stiletto heel.

I have never travelled with Liverpool supporters either in excursion trains or ordinary ones, but to hear them in wrath behind the goal convinces one that they can be a dangerous lot when loose *en masse*. It must be something in their cosmopolitan psychology, the element of Irish, Scottish, and English in their make-up which sends their tempers racing until they return to a state of childhood when they must smash and smash and smash and break and break, all for the Kop.

I have travelled with excursion trains to watch Chelsea and have come back seeing them beaten, but the reaction has only been a tense silence, a grim lethargy in which sad chins remain sunk in the pink classified editions of Northern newspapers, trying to dissect disaster.

The trouble with Chelsea supporters, until recently, was that they rarely cheered their team and there was no one among them ever who believed a toilet pan should be wrenched out of the floor for the sake of the club. I can't imagine a Chelsea native on his knees pulling at the pan, his chin on the enamel, tugging and pulling and cursing the afternoon's referee. They are a milder lot.

Chelsea have never had a Kop and there have been far too many supporters like 'Shorty' who wrote to the *News Chronicle* in 1950: 'I have been a regular paying visitor to Stamford Bridge for many, many moons but owing to my stature (only 5ft 3ins) I never see much of the match. Why do I go? It is because that, no matter how much of the game is blocked from my view, there is the satisfaction in feeling that I have not missed much.'

Chelsea seem to be getting more support now that success glows on them, but they have a long way to go to achieve the terrifying sound that hovers on the crest of an attack at White Hart Lane, or Old Trafford, or Anfield.

The great grandfather of sound, at Hampden Park, can still be as fearsome as ever, making visiting players pale and sick with that feeling that each one of the 120,000 is a spear aimed for his stomach.

We have rarely had the same sound at Wembley, apart from when the Scots come down with Tam O'Shanters pulled down over their ears and beer bottles sticking out of their pockets, and to a lesser extent, when the Irish and Welsh come.

The raucous volume of sound rarely swells in the same way for England, although I remember the roar in the rain when we beat Spain 4-2 at Wembley, in 1960, a sound of context to the placid state in which an English crowd often watches their team. Recently the English spectator took to booing his side – an extraordinary state of affairs. Mr. Ramsey's new tactics, 4-3-3, displayed at Wembley in February 1966, against West Germany, in preparation for the World Cup, made the spectators bellow with derision; so what could the English team expect in the World Cup finals?

What the crowd wanted, of course, was the popular high ball slung into the goalmouth from the deep, or the quick

'Get-rid-of-it' thump from the defense. They couldn't understand the build-ups, which, often monotonous and restricted to midfield, were not a sustaining pleasure. So the crowd booed.

What England could do with are more supporters of the West Ham type, who flooded the stadium with sheer joyous sound ('I'm Forever Blowing Bubbles'), when they beat Munich in the European Cup-winners Cup, in a classic final in May 1965; or the supporters of Tyneside who came down to Wembley in 1951, 1952 and 1955, and whirred the Blaydon Races sound all over North London. But it is strange that when England are out there, the crowd in the Wembley bowl often treats them almost as a group of distant insects.

What happens to all those pajama-clad men, women and children, who travel each Saturday out of town to watch their own sides, scarves wrapped round their necks like pythons, heads of their heroes scattered on badges on their chests, as they travel with their team on and on through the fields and towns and more fields. What happens to their voices when England come out of the tunnel at Wembley? A muted squeak.

And yet the English are a race of football fanatics, who travel to watch Queens Park Rangers play Swindon at Swindon, with the temperature below freezing, and the players themselves not really anxious to play, or stand huddled on the snow-bound terraces of Tranmere watching their own, sweet Brighton.

What a fanatical operation this supporters' club can be, so clamped in brotherhood and fraternity that the clubs themselves feel embarrassed at the pressures brought to bear on them, especially if they are financially in the poorer bracket.

The supporters clubs do a tremendous amount raising funds and so on, but sometimes a supporter feels that his own energies, which he had dispensed in following a club, means that he can automatically sway the board of a parent club. It doesn't of course. A supporter can travel millions of miles in defence of his team but that doesn't necessarily mean he has a say when things go wrong.

The bond between football clubs and supporters' clubs, in the higher echelons, is one of polite understanding, but a bond kept at a safe distance by the parent club. But when it comes to the crunch, a supporters' club won't have much say about a transfer or a new manager.

Many supporters' clubs are given their own private corner in the club programme, to state their recent adventures and the sagas of travel can sometimes be extraordinary, like this piece written in a Queens Park Rangers programme, shortly after they had been knocked out of the Cup 6-1 by the eventual finalists, Burnley, in 1962:

'SUPPORTERS' CORNER – HOME SWEET HOME!

'To travel nearly six hundred miles in eight days in support of one's team, only to see them concede ten goals and score two, has been the somewhat harassing experience of hundreds of Rangers' supporters these last two Saturdays.

'It is therefore good to be back at Loftus Road and gratifying to know that our travels afield will not be resumed until next month, for of course, we have another home fixture next Saturday.

'It is not often we bemoan our fate, but it certainly seems that Dame Fortune was very much with our opponents in Lancs and Hants.

'No one will 'crib' at the ultimate result of our Cup-tie against the Division 1 leaders, for they are a very good combination indeed. But to lose by five clear goals seemed a little unjust and hardly a true reflection of the game as a whole. The rather harsh penalty decision against us and 'own goal', was undoubtedly the turning point in a game in which our lads gave a very good account of themselves.

'It was heartening to see a splendid turn-out of supporters to Burnley. Despite the grim weather of a few days previously, hundreds made their way to Lancashire by road, rail and air.

'The rail party made their presence felt in no uncertain manner on arrival at Burnley, for headed by a one-man-band in the person of Jim Edmonds of Willesden, and much to the delight of the local inhabitants, they marched their way to the football ground. The co-operation of the good-natured Lancashire 'bobbies' did much to facilitate their progress at traffic junctions!

'The coach party had a very fair journey, arriving in good time for the game. A few fog patches were encountered on the return trip, but some excellent driving by our regular 'pilots' ensured that all were safely deposited at Shepherds Bush by 2 a.m. on Sunday morning.

'Over at London Airport, the twenty air adventurers (including this scribe) had a nail-biting experience, for the scheduled 8.50 a.m. flight to Manchester finally left at 12.34, much to the ultimate relief of the twenty, who were beginning to wonder if they would ever see the game at all! Again, some intrepid driving by our Cheshire coach driver over the hills and dales of Lancashire and we were safely in our seats just before the players came on to the field.

'The return trip was less eventful and after an excellent (if none-too-leisurely) dinner at the Queens Hotel, Manchester, we were airborne around 8.30 p.m. and back at Heathrow at 9.20. A coach quickly conveyed us back to Shepherds Bush.

'In all an adventurous, but none-the-less enjoyable day, despite the morning's set backs and made even more pleasant by the understanding and high good humour of the gallant twenty, who, although comparative strangers to each other in the morning, were all firm friends by the evening.'

For these supporters who became 'firm friends' on these incredible journeys, or enemies (as was the case with two Swansea supporters I saw outside the Peterborough ground after a Cup tie, trying with bloody success to bust each other's noses), there are always the long, fatiguing build-ups towards the game, the long trips back drunk with success; or the cold waiting in depressed grounds scribbling wild, insulting poetry on the far-away peeling walls of regional waiting rooms.

I can see the trains slicing through the countryside, visiting teams playing cards in a neat, tight square, younger supporters hovering behind them with their autograph books, older supporters travelling, often with a workmate, mumbling over their Roast Beef and Yorkshire about the day's prospects, men who can roar on the terraces, 'Get bleeding knotted, Eusebio', sipping their horrible, lukewarm soup with genteel little flicks of the wrist, and occasionally letting their eyes wander with huge astonishment over Clement Freud, the journalist and gourmet, in the process of ordering a bottle of British Rail Macon, a look of dumbfounded nausea on his face at the first sip, big eyes popping, staring.

At the terminal a rush of bodies to the ticket entrance, and if the ground is close, and the floodlight pylons can be seen straining their necks over the mist, the supporters run all the way, clattering through the tiny narrow streets which zig-zag towards the ground. At Northampton, Leicester, and Birmingham, these streets drag you back into the past when Dad came back from the front with mud on his puttees, or street lamps flickered with the shadows of the unemployed standing under them.

Down at the local hotel the team have lunch and a pep talk, the fans outside the door with the inevitable autograph books. After the game, the players stand on the platform signing autographs, with more gusto if they have won, and when they reach London or Manchester late that night, their followers shuffle along beside them shouting 'Denis Law, Denis Law,' or 'Sack Billy Wright.' Then the stations at midnight absorb the and the crowds disappear with the dust of foreign terraces still on their toes, disappear alongside newly married couples who have been picked up on the way by the same train and have been discreetly picking confetti out of each other's ears in a far corner, to the supporters strains of 'Roll me Over'.

The crowds disperse into the night but they will be there on their own grounds the following week, on the same trips of terrace which they regard as their second home. Some men die on these strips and are carried away stiff, a palish yellow glow on their faces, past the pitch at which they have stared for so many years, and all they get is a one paragraph mention in the evening news-papers: 'A man collapsed and died at the West Ham-Nottingham forest match this afternoon.'

But the living remain making the sound, as they will always do. And if they say that supporters are rougher now and less tolerant and more vicious, it is not strictly true. Before the First World War when every spectator wore a cloth cap and looked like a worker, and the players came on the field with beer in their bellies, there were plenty of raucous incidents and players and referees were often mobbed.

It was the same during the Twenties, Thirties and the Forties. And in the late Forties watching Millwall could be as hair-raising as being behind the goal at Elland Road or Goodison Park now. As the roar of the crowd swells into a crescendo, and toilet paper drifts languidly across the goalmouth, look back at the warning Millwall Football Club put out during the 1949-50 season after a bit of bother down at 'The Den'. It was addressed to men, who out of habit, knew how to respond to military orders:–

'DON'T DO IT CHUMS'

DON'T ever invade the playing pitch – keep your seats and places on the terraces – keep off the grass.

IF you do – trouble will ensue – offenders will be evicted from the Den and permanently denied admission thereto.

DON'T throw soil, cinders, clinkers, stones, bricks, bottles, cups, fireworks or other kinds of explosives, apples, oranges, etc. on the playing pitch during or after a match.

IF you do you are liable for eviction, prosecution and permanently denied admission to the Den.

DON'T forget that their are ladies and children in your midst.

DON'T barrack, utter filthy abuse, or cause any physical violence to the referee and his Linesman inside or outside the Den.

IF you do the Football Association will impose severe penalties upon the Club and close the Den either for a long period or permanently.

IF the ground is closed for a period, we will not be allowed to play during the period stated on any other ground within a radius of twelve miles from the Den.

IF you are not conversant with the rules and instructions of the Football Association, the following will enlighten you:

ANY MISCONDUCT TOWARDS A REFEREE AWAY FROM THE FIELD OF PLAY WILL BE DEALT WITH AS IF THE OFFENCE HAD BEEN COMMITTED ON THE FIELD.

DON'T barrack, utter filthy abuse, or molest in any manner players of the visiting team.

IF you do you are liable to eviction, prosecution, and permanently denied admission to the Den.

DON'T barrack, utter filthy abuse, or molest in any manner the players of the Millwall Football Club.

IF you do you are liable to eviction, prosecution, and per-manently denied admission to the Den.

DON'T assemble in small or large numbers on the streets adjacent to the Den.

IF you do you will be dispersed by the Police, and for certain alleged offences, such as obstruction, disturbance or breach of the peace, may render yourselves liable to prosecution.

DON'T deface or remove the Warning Notices which are posted within the Den.

IF you do trouble will ensue.

DON'T ever forget that the Directors of the Club reserve the 'RIGHT OF ADMISSION'.

Think on this: 'As a bird is known by its chirp, so is a man by his conversation.'

The future of this old club depends entirely upon your good conduct. To be – or not to be – it is up to you to 'PLAY THE GAME'…'

Was it all so different then?

XXIII. Northampton: The County Ground

Northampton Town, nicknamed the 'Cobblers', came up from The Third Division to the Second in 1963, from the Second to the First in 1965, and went back to the Second in 1966, but their grateful supporters and their grateful town never really left the Third. It was all too much for them, the supporters with their rustic benevolence, their cheerful intolerance, their blatant naivety. Sitting in that tiny, cramped, cow-shed stand, next to farmers with rosettes, on which fat babies carried 'the Cobblers' painted across their plastic navels was an experience which suggested minor football or perhaps not even football, a local meet outside a country pub with Farmer Brown farting on his hunter through too much brandy the night before.

I got to know Northampton when they were in the Second Division, and later in the First, and while the football was always robust and lively, the proceedings never became serene; poise and tradition found at Manchester on the Old Trafford ground or at Anfield or at St James' Park inflicted itself on the atmosphere like walking into the Louvre or the Vatican Museum. It was rural, funny, and sometimes, you wanted to scream with irritation.

As the matches become more and more important, the town couldn't cope. The traffic bulging the centre of the town half-an-hour before the kick-off, was wedged in a solid block. The queues of men with caps like pudding basins and grey mackintoshes shuffled forward into the special buses and made weird groaning noises when somebody jumped the queue.

I asked the way on an afternoon in 1965 and a policeman said: 'Are you from Birmingham?' 'No.' 'Well if you had been I would have told you the ground was in the opposite direction.' He told me the ground was over a mile away and I'd have to take one of the specials. I queued up in that block outside the church, a pretty church which symbolizes an ancient town. The war memorial has a painted Union Jack on it made of concrete. It was the market day and women with baskets pushed by banging our rumps with their baskets full of detergent. They have come in from the country and they regarded the waiting queue as being Dad's lot.

In a red bus, a shambling box on wheels, a man said to me: 'You follow the Villa.' 'No. I'm neutral.' 'Well you look like one of them. Up the Cobblers.' The bus conductress with peroxide hair and a foreign accent, grappled with a young thoroughbred with pink cheeks and a Northampton rosette. 'Get off boy. We're full, full, boy.' She held him in her arms nursing him like a naughty child. The youth appealed to us with his eyes which were yellow and moist.

The conductress heaved him off and the bus started in jerks and then slowed to a crawl and we passed shops bulging with rustic affluence, toothbrushes, suspenders, washing machines, and on past little red houses guarding narrow streets and ending in darkness – Victoria Road, Raglan Street, Wilberforce Street, streets where soldiers in red once marched and Yeomanry mustered.

A big advertisement on an adjacent bus: Vast Selection of Flowering Trees and Shrubs. Two youths examined each others shoes, casuals: 'Not high enough,' said the shaggy one. 'See these heels, they're an inch too short. When I walk I want to walk tall.'

'I think we'll get another win,' said a man. Second win – Northampton had only won one game out of seventeen, as their poor league position showed but they were triers and

Aston Villa could be beaten. It seemed hard on these support-ers that a win was as important as their wage packets. They sat in the bus with their claret scarves chewing their lips and making nervous pronouncements because they had been starved of success, and below it all they felt self-conscious at being supporters of a poor, non-aristocratic team. They were deeply sensitive but although their side was terribly vulnerable, they couldn't see it and didn't want to.

The bus moved through purple-tinged parks and more little red streets and the crowd on each side of us grew into platoons, then companies, then battalions, then armies, then we were there. The man with three chins next to me wheezed with excitement, the bus shuddered; there was a rush to the open plug hole of the bus and men were dancing away, moving faster than at an time during the working week.

Down a street guarded by starving shrubs, past the 'Spion Kop' entrance where craniums stuck out against the chilly blue sky like death heads.

The ground was an anti-climax. No tall terraces here, no feeling of enormous tension which one gets staring down from the press box at White Hart Lane or Goodison Park, no enormous, ominous, overpowering Spion Kop but a small hummock. And the ground was really for cricket anyway. Across the other side of the pitch was a score board with wick-ets 0, Bowlers 0, Batsman 1, 0. On the other side a thin red line of spectators, no higher than a cavalry charge, certainly not a First Division crowd. Some of them sing 'When the Saints Go Marching In.'

Northampton Town Football Club is associated with Northampton Town Cricket Club. The intrinsic qualities which make up top football are not here. The Press Box, based in a long, glass box at the top of the stand was full when I arrived, so I had to sit in a seat in the row below. There was no room for the knees, the man in front of me allowed me to tuck my knee caps into his shoulder blades and they were warm and quivered occasionally.

Villa took the field in all white, moving nonchalantly down to the goal where the spectators were least. They rubbed their hands together and posed for photographs. Then the home team were out, a rusty roar bringing them on, big men in claret with large waists and behinds. 'Your best chance for a big prize! The Daily Dip and Cobblers Bobbers, £700 a week,' said a notice in the programme.

'I've lost my gloves,' said a woman in front of me. She is wizened and gnarled from too much housework. On her right her pretty daughter with long black hair and a yellow and black college scarf squeezed her hands together. Farmers edged forward brandishing their canes, full of best bitter. 'I've lost me gloves,' says the woman. 'Can't see them, mum,' said the girl looking up at her mother's crutch.

The ref was on and the captains tossed up. A low hum of expectation. 'Northampton won't go down,' said a man. 'They tackle hard, that's what the Continentals never do no more, they never tackle. It ruins the bloody game. Football's hard tackling. Hop the Cobblers.'

They were off. The footballers were big truncheons, the game was rough, jagged, unpleasant. Villa made a slow start which teams often do on this ground. A Fulham player had told me that the tiny ground acted like 'bromide' on a visiting team. 'You don't want to play football on that pitch. It doesn't look like a football. You don't even want to lie down and have a quiet wank.'

Villa went through the motions but they weren't interested and Hall scored two violent goals against them in the ninth and tenth minute.

The crowd in the stand who only saw one team gibbered with enthusiasm. Their team was the greatest; Hall, Di Stefano. 'I've lose me gluves,' said the woman again, and then when a Villa player tackled a hero she said: 'Don't push, don't push.'

'At him,' said the college girl.

The game grew worse. Some of the tackling was so aggressive that one marvelled at the strength of the human limb. Foley of Northampton, a tough, garrulous Irishman, tangled with Deakin, the fiery left-half of Villa. They rolled on the floor and in the sudden silence you could hear flesh slithering against flesh.

'Dirty beast, dirty swine,' shouted a farmer.

'I've lost me gloves,' said the woman unconcerned.

The men were pulled apart and the referee without much concern awarded a bounce up.

'Dirty swine, swine, send the swine HOFF HOFF HOFF,' shouted the farmer.

But the crowd were not quick to join in. Their fellow was partly to blame. But in the main they were partisan and saw only good in their own side and applauded only their team. They are the same as any crowd but more so. They did not appreciate football, only successful football played by their own side.

At the end of the game, with Villa losing 2-1, the referee played six extra minutes because of injuries. The crowd resented it, the woman still looking for her 'gluves', gave up and squeezed her lips together with suspense, her daughter hurled back her thick, black hair and entreated the referee to stop: 'For Christ sake stop it ref.' The game was on and Coe, the Northampton goalkeeper did splendidly, groping the ball and finding it, pushing it into his stomach and punting it way down field. The whistle blew and the crowd ecstatically invaded the pitch.

The night had blackened, the atmosphere was raw but happy with victory. The crowd talked about Coe – 'He must stay' – the woman and her daughter were sucked away towards the stairs, with them suddenly was an inconspicuous man in tweeds who said nothing during the game.

The players forced their way through the crowd and there were boos for the referee who tore into the players' entrance, his head bobbing from side to side like an alarmed tortoise.

The streets revealed nothing but retreating figures, the lamps around the stadium were flickering candles at High Mass, no more than that strength. In the directors room we could have a glass of scotch or a cup of tea and a sandy biscuit. A young woman, motherly, handsome, peered down at her cup of tea. The woman wore a heavy coat which one wanted to tell her not to wear because the pink didn't suit her. I left the room and made for the bus stop. The crowd had thinned and the bus queue was short. But again the buses dragged along into the Town centre past groups of young Villa supporters squeaking blasts on their hooters – Da, Da, Dee, Dee, Da Da, Dee Dee Dee.

In the bus I wrote my report. It didn't come easy, a block or two, a sentence, another block, a look at the watch, a cigarette, a sentence, a cigarette, a sentence, the bus has nearly reached the town centre. It wasn't a game where a luscious report lies afterwards to be picked and deposited without a second thought. It was an average game which pleased the locals because their side had made a rare win, but their enthusiasm, reflected through cheerful whoops on the bus, left one sorry that there is nothing better for them. A woman broke the monopoly of post mortem: 'I hear they are opening a Take Away Your Steak place,' she said. 'Not heard of it,' said her husband.

Northampton were a big team, susceptible to a quick pass through the middle, susceptible in fact to anything original. But Villa without the injured Phil Woosnam, had not been constructive or original and had deserved to lose. You cannot play a five man attack forward line in this era all running forward like bullocks and expect to beat a retreating defence with two men marking a man. Villa had responded like an ageing picador goaded and defeated. But it hadn't been the same with other sides.

The bus stopped and I walked the half mile to Northampton Castle Station. The evening had become cold and lonely; women sat in coffee shops staring out vacantly as I passed. In a station booth, I telephoned my report. The telephonist took it down giving a vague sigh after each pause. Outside a group of Villa supporters are making a racket as they read their green, classified edition.

When the train came in it was impossible to get a seat. Thousands of boys crowded into the first class carriages when they couldn't get a seat elsewhere. The train moved out slowly and moved after a number of stops in the general direction of Watford Junction. At the first stop down the line some of the kids got out with their autograph books and caps and I sat down with a family in a first class carriage. It was uncomfortably hot in the carriage and there was a heavy smell of sweat and newspaper.

A mother and young daughter sat next to me eating crisps and watching the young man with glasses opposite, he had a thin nervous mouth and he hid behind an enormous Northampton rosette which splashed mauve all over his undeveloped chest. He kept his knees together like a woman and sometimes his head made an hysterical effort to be drawn down into his body. His adam's apple made sudden darts downwards.

Opposite, his mother offered him a crisp and he said, 'No Mum'. Beside him is a girl with wheat coloured hair and a pleasant, almost beautiful face, wearing a black jersey and black slacks. She made pronouncements: 'While you did the shopping we went to that boring game. Preferred to have gone shopping. Soppy footballers.'

The young man brooded in silence. Was the girl his lover or sister? I examined them for traces of affection but there was none. 'Your socks are filthy,' said the older girl looking across at the younger one. She was a bully. The mother murmured: 'They were clean this morning,' 'But they're filthy now,' said the girl. 'Filthy dirty. She looks filthy, don't you look filthy.' 'My socks are dirty, not filthy,' said the younger one. 'Oh leave her alone.' Said the mother.

The youth started sliding the door backwards and forwards

so that cold draughts of air came billowing in. He got more and more frantic until the older girl said: 'What you doing?'

'Doing? Doing nothing.'

'All that soppy football,' said the girl.

They could be lovers, or courting furtively perhaps. The youth sniffed his rosette and caught my eye. He withdrew immediately from the glance and picked up the green, classified edition. He read it but made no pronouncement about the game he had seen although the match was reported in the gravest detail: 'HALL SHOOTS COBBLERS AHEAD.'

The youth looked across at his mother. She was wearing a headscarf.

'Saw something which I never saw before,' he said. 'A ball going through the net.'

'What?' said the girl, 'can't hear you.'

'A ball going right through the net.'

'Wha?' Said the girl looking at him, chin out, plunging mercilessly in. 'Wha?'

'A net with the ball going through it. The ball went in the net and out the other side.'

Silence.

I thought back to the game and couldn't remember the ball going through the net at any time. They went on eating crisps now and the noise was a continuous crackle like a bonfire. The ticket collector arrived and found the family hadn't got first class tickets. 'This happens all the time on this line,' he said loudly.

'The question is do you mind them being in here, sir.'

He looked across at me. 'No I don't mind.'

'Well if you don't mind then it's alright for you to stay,' said the ticket collector and the youth sits tight, expressionless. The mother said: 'Well we're getting off at Watford Junction.'

When the ticket collector went off she said; 'Didn't like him.'

'Always the same on this line,' said the youth. 'They come

in and try and turn you out. But the second class is always full.'

'The older girl said: Well, I wouldn't have gone anyways.'

At Watford Junction the Northampton supporters and their group left the carriage and the train broke down for an hour. During that time I tried to remember when the ball went through the net but couldn't recall the moment.

XXIV. Tangier

Ahmed was a Moroccan painter, but he couldn't read or write. I met him in Dean's Bar, in Tangier, one evening when he was as usual about to do a favour for a wealthy American lady.

'Come for a drink in my room tomorrow,' he said. 'I'll tell you about Tangier.'

We met at noon at his studio, which was in the basement of a solid, white apartment house bordering the beach. Lilting, twangy Arab music drifted across the room, which was full of red canvasses, strangely mystical and pleasing, and photographs of Western women either in bathing costumes or in cocktail dresses. I was very hot and I had a feeling of slight doom as one does sometimes at noon. The room which I had entered to Ahmed's grunt, was in semi-darkness, and strange shapes and visions filled the part not lit by the stabbing light of the curtain I had lifted with my nose.

'Are you there, Ahmed?' I said.

'Yes, the woman has gone.'

'How are you?'

'I am well. Come and play football.'

'Marvellous. Where?'

'On the beach. We have two teams. But first read me the letter from a woman in America.'

It was hard to see Ahmed. There was in the corner of the room a streak of yellow colour which was the outline of a torn and battered blanket, maybe a carpet, and on it a naked form wearing what seemed to be a Coca Cola cap. At least the words of Coca Cola were attached to the skull, sagging down on a pair of knees; long graceful arms circled round a bulbous pair of kneecaps.

One of the hands extended towards me with an envelope and I took it, moving back towards the light. The letter was from Salt Lake City, and was headed 'Sweet Ogre' with aggressive biro. I read out the letter to a man who couldn't read or write, but was a very good painter, and he said, 'It sounds good.' The letter was stacked with placid endearments. 'Oh darling, your strong arms still engulf me. I feel you crush me. Oh, sweet ogre, you stifle me, Bill comes home these days and I just don't feel the same. What I feel for you is something personal as if that day on the beach was a day in which nobody, simply nobody else was alive except you sweet ogre and me.'

'What does she mean,' said Ahmed veering up into the fresh-water light so that his chin jutted out, jaundiced coloured in the rays of the sun, the Coca Cola sign on his paper cap turned blood red.

'She loves you, one of a million.' I said.

'She was a good woman,' said Ahmed. 'There she is.'

He pointed to a photograph pinned on the wall. A tough, Nordic looking blonde started out at us, her bikini stretched over her stoutish body which gave a far more noticeable bulge to her belly. Ahmed lit a kief cigarette and incense flooded the room. 'You want one,' he asked, thrusting out a block of wood on which four or five cigarettes were stacked.

'Not if we're playing football.'

'We play football. Some of my relatives from Fez.'

Ahmed got off the bed and walked straight out into the open air through the curtain. He wasn't naked, a small yellow g-string hung round his hips, a crab-like body burnt by the sun, the Coca-Cola cap pushed down on his head. He had a strong, prominent face, a youth of about twenty-three. 'That woman was a woman,' he said as we padded across the hot sand towards the sea. 'She could roll and roll. And nights Mr. took us to nightclubs. She bought two of my paintings. She was a woman.'

We walked up to the beach where a small group of figures were standing in a group near a pair of goalposts stuck unevenly in the sand. There were about fifteen men in the group, ten Europeans and six Moroccans all wearing bathing costumes or shorts, and of various physical make-up, ages ranging from forty to eighteen.

Ahmed threw away his cigarette and steered me into the group. There was a strong discussion going on in high-pitched Arabic and German. Ahmed said: 'You play with me.'

It was a gusty, hot day; figures withered glossy on the sand in repose; over the beach, Tangier climbed zigzagging upwards in the heat in slabs of melting white, and the sea on the other side of us was stark blue and crammed with bobbing heads.

We sorted ourselves out into some sort of opposition, which turned out to be eight-a-side, and from what I could see the players were either very fit and locals, or very fat and out of condition. There were three Germans in our line-up with corpulent bellies, midget bikinis, from which lashings of curly tufted hair ambled forth, bald craniums shining with red sun-burn, and glinting teeth. Ex-S.S?

We were off.

Ahmed on kief was very dangerous, a natural ball player, who had played with some distinction for a local side.

He weaved forward over the sand beating two bloated English soldiers who had told me they were from Gibralter, and I thought as he moved on of Pele and what he had done a few weeks before to Sweden. But when he shot at goal the shot was saved by the most astonishing man, a Moroccan of about sixteen with a shaven head, so brown that the skin had turned almost white, thin, tree-shaped legs, long arms, a woman's red bathing costume covering his nipples, a pair of basket-ball boots with no soles, a pair of sunglasses with only the frames, a mouth full of ivory teeth. He took Ahmed's shot like Brazil's

Gylmar, accelerating into the top corner of the goal.

'Er, er, errr,' he moaned as he sank to the ground clutching the ball.

'He doesn't talk, he doesn't hear,' said Ahmed strolling back. The 'keeper gave the ball a mighty kick and fell on his stomach. It landed at my feet and I flicked it with some difficulty, considering the size of dinner the night before, to one of the German trio. The three went off together making strange noises which sounded like *Zieg Heil! Zieg Heil! Zieg Heil!* Until – corpulent and full of wind – they reached the deaf and dumb 'keeper who hurled himself at their final combined poke administered by three fleshy big toes going out together and going clang on the leather, and held the ball gibbering: 'err, errr, errrr.'

'He's a nutcase,' said one of the English soldiers standing picking at his medallion, his khaki shorts hung up above his pot belly.

The football wasn't very good. I was conscious of players running very slowly and making gruff noises, but our team was on the attack most of the time, the German trio moving forward in selfish jerks, waggling their hips, barking orders, the three who would be up around the Casbah later that night looking for a bit of *Mein Liebe* and Ahmed not really very interested, but playing the game naturally and beautifully, and the deaf and dumb goalkeeper hurling himself to stop the shots we rained at him.

Then I got away on the seaside so that the water splashed my feet and the ball, centered beyond the deaf and dumb 'keeper and one of the bald Germans got up and headed into the goal. The sight was unbelievable. The scorer leapt into the air and joined his other fat friends in a wild jig, the deaf and dumb 'keeper stuck his nose into the sand and started having a fit, he banged his knuckles onto the hard sand, 'Err, errr, errr.' Then he was up and chasing the scorer and kicking him up the backside. Ahmed looked on calmly as the three Germans caught hold of the gibbering 'keeper with wild laughs and cackles and the 'keeper began screaming.

'He does this every day,' Ahmed said. 'He likes football like I like women.'

But he was no longer looking. His eyes had wandered to a woman passing about fifty yards away like one of those aircraft which drone down for a landing at London Airport, undercarriage down, calm and safe.

She was rolling along with a thick black bathing costume, a black turban, books under her arm, colossal sunglasses on the top of her nose, and her chin up in the air. She paid no attention to the scuffle. The deaf and dumb 'keeper had broken loose from the crazy grasps of Deutschland and was hopping back to his goal, but the Germans had obviously had enough, marching off towards one of the smarter private beaches, roaring with laughter. The two English soldiers drifted away: 'Bloody nutcase. Let's have a beer.'

Ahmed was standing there still watching the woman who was about 100 yards away moving up the beach and away from us. 'I will meet you later,' he said and ran off across the sand in leisurely running motion until he became a speck gradually linking up against another speck of flesh.

The deaf and dumb 'keeper still had a few of us to play with, but he didn't make any more scenes when he was beaten. He made some wonderful saves and chuckled to himself each time he held the ball.

When I came off the pitch and went over to a beach café for a drink, Ahmed was sitting there with the woman. She looked solid and presentable, about thirty-five, and her eyes seemed to burn through her dark glasses. 'I'm Amelia Slade from St Louis,' she said. 'Pleased to meet you.'

Ahmed grinned.

XXV. Torquay: Plainmoor

The centre-forward of Tottenham and Scotland looked at himself in the mirror and seemed pleased with what he saw. He put a comb through his black hair for the last time and, as it came out of the neat thatch, he gave the comb a little upward jerk of satisfaction, to celebrate.

I stood against the urinal and glanced back at him. For a moment he caught my eye and his look was cold but distant, a little tense as if the game ahead was not one he was looking forward to; a Cup-tie in which his side had everything to lose.

Alan Gilzean went out of the toilet into the barren corridors of a Torquay hotel. His team had just held a tactical talk and were moving off to play Torquay in a third round of the F.A. Cup.

But Torquay did not feel like a place where you would find Tottenham playing. The palms and shrubs and vast, servile hotels, hanging down over the sea were more a part of Hollywood of the Twenties and life long ago.

Gilzean was in the foyer preparing to leave with the team. He looked more like a civil servant than a footballer, tall and clerical in a dark suit. It didn't seem possible that he was one of the finest headers of the ball in football. Centre-forwards like Tommy Lawton or Dixie Dean always stood out, rough, bullet-headed and occasionally flexing their neck muscles. Gilzean stood there shyly as if he had just arrived on honeymoon.

At his side was Jimmy Greaves, chirpy and smiling for journalists: 'Hullo, hullo, how are you, Reg,' in front of more moody players like Billy Brown the goalkeeper. A game of cards in which the majority of the players had taken part was over, now it was *the* game which mattered. The footballers were a group apart, surrounded by old ladies thinking of death and middle aged couples pretending they were on dirty weekends.

Danny Blanchflower, now a journalist and commentator, in a smart overcoat, moved smoothly through the foyer. I waited for him to say 'Hullo thar,' but he avoided his advertising jargon.

People greeted him with affable smiles. Danny has a way with hangers on, mostly polite and affable. Outside the hotel swing doors, a group of fat men offered him a lift: 'Hullo Danny, want a lift, Danny? Get in, Danny.'

The team left for the ground. They pushed out of the swing doors carrying overcoats. They were followed by supporters carrying autograph books, and sad expressions to go with them, and one wondered if the team would loosen up on the field, because they didn't seem in the mood.

The massive Hotel Regal turned to normality. Outside on its lawns, winter – as mild as spring – had spread a blueish, ragged carpet over what was normally a sheet of pure green, and tall purple trees dripped moisture. An old woman snored in the lounge, her stick legs flung out over a flower-petalled sofa, waiting to be snapped; the hall porter was on the telephone gazing ahead with ice forming on his eyebrows. There was an enormous silence.

It didn't seem possible that a First Division football team was here in this resort, where people came to die and to lengthen their lives a little longer. But when I arrived at Plainmoor the crowd was squeezed like toothpaste into a small stadium, expectant, full-throated; a bull-ring compared to the silence of the big hotel. The band and a corps of drums of the Devonshire Regiment (First Rifle Volunteers) T.A. burst into 'Abide with Me'.

'Hold though thy Cross before my closing eyes;
Shine through the gloom, and point me to the skies;
Heaven's morning breaks, and earth's vain shadows flee;
In life, in death, O lord, abide with me!'

The programme said: 'Everyone is respectfully asked
please to join in the singing of 'Abide with Me' on this historic
occasion.'

There was a shy response. 'Well let them play it now. After
all, they won't be at Wembley,' said a cynical journalist.

The game itself did not turn out as expected. Torquay
scored the first goal, but Tottenham made the score 3-1 and
there it remained until five minutes before time, when the
Torquay centre-forward Robin Stubbs squeezed in two goals to
force a replay. The emotion showed on that occasion has few
parallels. A man pulled at my ears as the third goal went past
Bill Brown, his saliva dripping down my collar. In the press box
we struggled to make another note as arms and fingers veered
towards our noses. It was great cup-tie stuff, the perfect ending
for a little team.

But back in the big hotel where I rushed to write my report
they seemed unimpressed. Silence was still paramount, tea cups
tinkled, and there was a smell of talcum powder. In the writing
room I scribbled down a mass of words on hotel letter paper
watched by old women with hawkish eyes.

Torquay had achieved a moment of glory but half the
town did not appear to want to know. Up in the American bar
couples talked about their cars but when the barman mentioned
Torquay and Robin Stubbs they politely changed the subject.

The big hotel settled for a night, towers rising out of
clumps of trees, sleek cars crunching on the drive, settled for
a night without football. The Spurs are already away, having
been escorted by the police to a train at Newton Abbott after
the game. They left behind a knot of journalists and supporters
waiting for the midnight sleeper.

I phoned my report from the hotel and hurried out of
the solemnity of the foyer where the porter with icicles on his
eyebrows was still on duty.

In the harbor, small groups of Spurs supporters hung
around eating fish and chips and looking bored. It was a windy,
January night, and a tingling chill came off the sea. It was on
a cliff top that I found a hotel where I was told the food was
good and they served decent wine. Below was the sea, a sheet of
black, plate glass, and the town, with bowling alleys, a football
match which had been played, and a jovial hero called Robin
Stubbs splashed across the front pages of the football editions.

In the restaurant there was an eerie silence. A few couples
were sitting contemplating each other's elbows across the huge
expanse. A waiter showed me to a table near a panoramic
window, through which the lights of Torquay harbor were
burning like tiny bonfires.

At the next table was a man who resembled a cockerel,
jaunty, jerking his head slightly as he descended towards his
plate of smoked salmon; his tie was smart blue. His woman
was drowned in green chiffon and her necklace, made of white
beads, clung desperately to her jerky neck. They looked like
Londoners and they were.

'You were at the match today,' said the man calling across
at me. 'In the press box. I saw you. Well, what did you tell your
readers?'

'It was quite a finish,' I called back. Our voices sounded
catastrophic in the silence.

'Well I'm, my wife and I, are Spurs supporters,' said the
man, taking a long ostentatious sip of red wine. 'But we were
disappoint-ted in them today. They should never have allowed
that centre-forward in. They went to sleep. It was diabolical.'

His wife looked over at me but no expression crossed
her face, which remained strained and slightly aloof. She was
attractive and domineering in style, but she was obviously
fighting a waterfall of facial lines. I got the impression that she

could not move her face because of all the powder stuck like suet pudding to her cheeks.

A waiter who was pointing out to me some exquisite, vily expensive Burgundies on the wine list, heard the man talking about football. He turned and said softly to the Spurs supporter: 'I won the match ball in the supporters' club raffle today, sir.'

'Well, isn't that super,' said the man. 'Did you hear that,' he said to his companion. 'He won the match ball.'

'Super,' said the woman, 'the white one they played with?'

'Yes,' said the waiter. 'It's white. It was brown after the match but they cleaned it up for me. Don't you think Torquay were magnificent, sir?'

He looked at both of us forgetting my urgency to eat.

'Very brave, very brave,' said the man. 'They never knew when they were beaten. And that Stubbs has got class, real class. See him run off the ball, classy running, real class.'

'Torquay were really magnificent,' said the waiter. 'We're all very proud of them. I never see them mind you. And I don't know anybody who does but it's nice to think of a little team holding the giants sometimes.'

He took my order, which was a half-bottle of Volnay and said: 'Very good, a good choice, sir' and I saw a piece of smoked salmon catch the edge of the Spurs supporters' chin and fall back on the plate. He looked over at us: 'We are giants of course,' he said. 'But we don't mind losing our stride through the bravery of others occasionally. I have no doubt we'll win the reply, but we'll be honoured to have you with us at White Hart Lane. As my old friend Billy Nicholson will appreciate, the replay won't be a piece of cake.'

The waiter fluttered away beaming and looked over the man who said he was a Spurs supporter. His heavy horn-rimmed glasses and heavy lips gave him an engaging authority. 'We come down here for our holidays every year,' he said. 'So this was a nice extra break. They are very hospitable here you know. They don't bust your inside out with their cuisine. They take trouble.'

'Yes,' said his woman, 'they take trouble.'

'I've got a bone to pick with you press boys and many, mind you, are my friends. You don't give a fair picture always. I bet you say tomorrow Torquay were everything and Spurs were nothing. One-sided reporting I call it.'

'Well Torquay made a great fight of it. That is obviously the main story.'

'But it isn't always. Sometimes Spurs have played superb stuff and you press boys slate them. I can't see it really. I was talking to Dave Mackay about it and he said he felt the same way.

'And Jimmy felt the same way. And Cliff Jones gets mad about it too. We're all mad about it sometimes.'

'You know them well?'

'I know them all. They are very good friends of ours. My wife goes to the same laundry as Mrs. Greaves, and then there's the golf club. A lot of the boys come up there and we play a few holes. We're a jolly lot. Billy Nicholson couldn't have a better set of lads.'

My waiter brought a pleasing selection of produce for me to digest and the pheasant tasted delicious. 'You're having the pheasant,' said the man raising himself slightly on his chair and peering at my plate. 'We usually have the pheasant when we come down here but tonight we're having steak. We had pheasant last night.'

'It was super,' said his woman.

'What we need now is a class wing-half to replace Danny,' said the man. 'With Dave Mackay out with a broken leg we get caught out over and over again. Great gaps in the middle I could drive my Bentley through. Honestly I'm worried about the half-back line now. As I was telling Billy Nicholson the other day we need one more player and we'll be a great side. Jimmy wasn't trying today but he'll be on next Wednesday. And Gilzean's got what it takes. But you can't expect us to be great all the time, great some of the time but not all the time.'

A group of polite but exuberant revelers were celebrating in the corner. Suddenly they burst into 'Happy birthday dear Martha, happy birthday to you.' The Spurs supporters stood up and clapped. 'Happy birthday, happy birthday,' he called across the room. The group stared over and nodded their thanks. 'Glory, glory hallelujah,' somebody sang.

'And the Spurs go marching on,' said the Spurs supporter. We'll be marching on, you'll see.'

'Glory, glory hallelujah, and Torquay go marching on,' sang the birthday party. Almost at once the restaurant returned to its previous solemnity.

'Come along little woman,' said the Spurs supporter, 'let's have a waltz. Old stuff, we're old-fashioned, you see. But we like to twist sometimes.'

As he stood up with his woman her chiffon dress went hiss, hiss, against their table, and he said: 'You staying the weekend?'

'No, I'm catching the midnight train.'

'Well, good luck, that's a wicked journey. I like a bit of piece and quiet down here first. It's peaceful down here. But we'll be seeing you are White Hart Lane for the replay. See you in the Spurs dressing-room, afterwards maybe. By the way what paper will we have the honour of reading you inside?'

Later, as I went past the heavy, oakwood dance floor next to the dining room to get my taxi, I saw the Spurs supporter pushing his woman across the dance floor like Groucho Marx. The band was playing 'I'll get married in the Morning.' He waved and his woman turned and gave me a hazy smile.

On the way to Newton Abbott, I wondered what he meant about seeing me in the Spurs dressing room after the replay.

XXVI. We'll Never Know

'**H**endon League... Rawlplugs 5 Apex Reserves 6: a magnificent fighting rally in the closing stages gave Apex Reserves victory over their closest rivals in the chase for the Div 3 championship. After Rawlplugs had taken an early lead, Tony Shadbolt equalized and John Pamplin put the visitors ahead. In the second half Rawlplugs soon drew level and they regained the lead with a penalty, After Shadbolt had scored Apex's third, Rawlplugs put on the pressure and built up a 5-3 lead. In the closing minutes Clive Moyse and Shadbolt equalized and in the last seconds Colin Preen netted the winner.'

So said the *Finchley Times* one day, but we'll never really know what happened, apart from these bare, informative lines, as clinical as a city at dawn. Who was Shadbolt, the fiendish Shadbolt, who turned the game for Apex Reserves with his three goals? Was he thick or thin, did he move like a butterfly or a bull, did he scream with ecstasy when he equalized with that vital goal which made it 5-5?

Shadbolt, a good, solid name for a footballer; thick bulging knee caps, perhaps, with a jaw which munched gum; cool, blue eyes, dirt on white stockings, mud on the navel, clear headed, a little aggressive, a little garrulous, moody, but on this day, this afternoon, moving with grace and confidence, leaping in the air perhaps when his first equalizer sped in, coaxing the Apex Reserves back into the game. We'll never know.

Who were the crowd, a smattering of faces peeping out of dirty mackintoshes, voyeurs or addicts, odd partisans longing for the local, the sudden thrill that the game was a good one, that Rawlplugs had a chance, that Apex Reserves were coming in to win?

Did the wind howl across North London? Where was the game played (the report didn't say)? Were the conditions intolerable; was the game sporting, or mixed with wild obscenities; did the net hiss when the ball hit the net? Was there a raging fandango of pleasure when Apex Reserves scored their last minute winning goal? All this we do not know. We can only imagine the winning dressing room, a small stifled box full of pegs and one shower hissing in the toilet annex and the team naked and bellowing with pleasure, the smell of dirty socks, greasy shirts, bandages discarded in reels of tape; boots everywhere as profuse as seaweedy rocks. Mud, mud, mud, and one player perhaps sunk in glorious hibernation with his head in his hands; a woman waiting outside; a voice in the shower, 'Good old Tony,' a highly strung feeling of victory. 'What a goal, Colin.' 'Good auld Tony.' Noise, noise, noise, noise, and afterwards at a local, brown and light ales and the soft haircuts of the winning players linked round in a circle of fluff. 'Good auld Tony, you took 'em well Tony 'onest you did.' 'Well you set 'em up for me. I just cracked 'em in.' But was it like this? We'll never know, we'll never know beyond the report except that Apex Reserves won by 6-5 in the last seconds.

The losers' dressing room, macabre, yellow-faced players less anxious to strip, leaning on their kneecaps, wanting to pound their flesh in frustration, screaming inwardly, hating their team mates, why, oh, why? The men of Rawlplugs shattered, shattered men of Rawlplugs staring perhaps at the opposite wall with glazed eyes, Or were they cheerful, praising their colleagues' rally, cheerfully accepting their late slide? Do they rub themselves down with the look of languid men, wish they were not footballers at this moment, exposed to ridicule? Do they creep home to their wives and girl friends with dull, beaten faces asking only to sink into a settee and contemplate the tele and mutter, 'It was diabolical.' We'll never know.

The Sunday mornings after absorb these games; North London is silent, rows and rows of silent houses, streets silent, only a milk-man buzzing past, seagulls sagging on goalposts of local Co-operative Society grounds. The men of Apex Reserves perhaps slept late and woke with joy in their bellies; well they might bellow, 'Hullo, love', but we'll never know.

And the men of Rawlplugs may have woken up and stared at the ceiling and seen a dirty sky outside and thought: 'if only I had passed the ball to so and so instead of passing it to so and so,' and 'if', and 'if,' and 'if,' and 'hell'; We'll never know.

And we'll never know if Apex Reserves met the next day at a North London local with a pop group going in the background and pints of Guinness and bitter all round to celebrate and Shadbolt in the middle being toasted and Colin Preen who scored the winner. Or maybe they were teetotallers and took their game so seriously they didn't drink anything but orange juice and went out with their girlfriends and wives after lunch to the pictures and didn't talk about the game because they believed in being modest.

And the team from Rawlplugs: did they go out and dissect their defeat at the local with the traffic swishing by on ramps out of London towards the North, awful bitchy criticism through to closing time, or did they just forget the whole thing and say: 'Well, it was close. We'll win next week.'

Either way it doesn't matter. Footballers tend to be in a weird psychological state after a game, wildly effusive or moody as hell. We'll never know what really happened. But it is easy to imagine.

XXVII. Port Vale

The players had mushroom soup, the director had smoked salmon, the manager had a prawn cocktail. It was the manager, a dry, warm-eyed Scot, who did most of the talking.

The players sat by themselves picking gingerly at their food and murmuring in soft cockney. The manager, the director, the trainer sat at another table with a good view of Stoke railway station on a clear day. The director ate like a pig enjoying his day out, taking deep gulps at a glass of lager, a stout little man with heavy horn-rimmed glasses and a black executive suit. The manager fell behind with his prawn cocktail because he was doing all the talking and was still nibbling at a dampish prawn as the director began pushing back lumps of roast beef and Yorkshire.

The players could hardly be heard five yards away across the bleary red carpet of the hotel, a neat, vaguely unathletic bunch of lads dressed in neat suits with the top buttons of their light woolen casual shirts hanging against their bobbing Adam's apples.

The manager was talking about the side his Third Division club were taking on that day, which was Port Vale, at Vale Park, Burlem, Arnold Bennett country. They had invited me to join them as the only journalist covering the match from London.

'They're a hard side,' said the manager. 'And they don't lie down. Remember last September.'

'We were robbed,' said the director.

'Robbed, yes,' said the manager. 'But they impressed me.

They've got guts, especially the centre-forward. Larry's got to stand on him today. We usually get a point at Port Vale. Last year we would have got two, but Bill slung one in, in the last minute. The lad took a goal-kick and it only went a couple of yards out of the area. Their centre-forward lobbed the ball back and that was it.'

'Robbed again,' said the director.

'We need every point,' said the manager, a no-nonsense type with his own unswayable views. 'We can't make any mistakes now if we are to get promotion.'

'Tell 'em to go in 'ard,' said the director, his mouth full of Cheddar. 'We've got to get stuck in from the start. No mummy stuff.'

The manager gave a thin smile and nodded. He had been listen-ing to the director's advice on trains up from the South for two years now and he always responded politely, but it was his own decisions which mattered and he stuck by them.

A waitress, with a huge tear in her black stocking, ambled up to our table bringing cups of lukewarm coffee. When she leaned over her breasts made an upward jerk and the director winked.

'I've got a god tip for the 2.30 at Cheltenham, Kismet,' he said, '8 to 1.'

'The trainer, a quiet, former professional, a rustic-type, chipped in for the first time. 'Backed it meself, Mr. Lee.'

'Well you're onto a good one Bill. Kismet's a stayer, he's a beauty. The restaurant manager at the Cumberland gave me the tip last week. He's rarely wrong, rarely.'

Some of the players started filing out of the restaurant rubbing their crew cuts with unnecessary sweeps of the hand. It was time to go. The manager offered me a lift in the team coach.

In the foyer the manager had a few whispered words with the team while the director took me aside. 'You must wish you were at Old Trafford today. But we have our fun on these trips.

They're a nice bunch of lads. I'll be chuffed if we get promotion. They'll be potty about it down at the golf club.'

We filed out to the coach. A roaring gale was blowing over the town carrying stray bits of snow which whirled like white feathers in and out of dark doorways and the entrance of the station shunting yard.

We climbed into the coach which had the name of our club on a window. The younger players, some chewing gum, sat in an expressionless group at the front while the older ones, the left-back, the goalkeeper and the inside-left sat in the rear with the manager, the director and the trainer. The bus moved off ponderously through the narrow streets.

Some of the clubs supporter's stood waving at the entrance of the hotel as we pulled away, their scarves growing further and father away until a twist in the road blanked out their patriotic, Cockney fervour.

It was out in the vast barren, hilly desert of the potteries that we felt strangers, surrounded by the giant slag heaps, a canyon dwarfing a stage coach. The landscape was grey, blackened, a multitude of cinders blotching the setting. Along the winding road the bus spluttered, pulling the enemy to the field.

When we arrived the crowd had only just started to arrive. They speckled the terraces and those in the entrance gave a mild boo as the players got out. The freezing gale howled round the ground and the players hunched their shoulders as they went to the dressing rooms. At the officials entrance in the main stand there was a smell of disinfectant coming from the showers. The director was talking racing to a Port Vale official he knew. 'I know it's going to be Kismet,' he said.

The ground began to fill, spectators huddling in congested, ragged blocks behind the two goals as the wind battered and beat them. In the press box which was in a hut with a long glass window at one corner of the ground, the local men were assembling their telephones and talking about the latest dressing news at Port Vale. The London side were hardly referred to except when the team changes came up.

When the London side came out there was an eerie silence, the bumping of the wind and one wondered where their supporters had got to. A minor cackle of joy greeted Port Vale lumbering out onto a park they knew as well as their own mattresses.

Those London athletes looked different now, as they kicked in down our end, sturdy men well greased and streamlined in technicolour strip, men oiled for combat, no longer men in simple suits, staring at you with the placid indifference of clerks behind an office desk.

So there was a game, and the Port Vale centre-forward was indeed a menace, as the London manager had prophesised, putting his side in front early on. It was a game in which the ball had to be hit hard in the gale, the gale often winning so that the two goalkeepers had to change direction at a sharp diversion.

It was a bone-biting game, choppy, with the ball hitting flesh and making a slap slap sound as it came off stomach muscles and chests. The London side grew more and more positive and when their centre-half got a grip on the Port Vale centre-forward and their two wingers took up the running, past two slow Port Vale backs the game swung round and goals came from the visitors. When the referee blew the final whistle the London side had two more points in their safe and I visualized smiles.

Hail was pinging against the players coach as I came up after phoning my copy. The director was already inside all screwed up as if the cold had crucified him. 'I told you Kismet would do it,' he said breathing hard. 'He's got in by a head, Crickey! It was blowing, wasn't it.'

'You did well.'

'I'm proud of the lads,' he said. 'Proud, Larry stayed on that centre-forward. He didn't like it, did he? And I haven't seen such fair running on a park this season as Enoch and Boris did today.'

The team came out of the main stand and climbed into the coach. The manager had a tight smile on his face which was disguised by a frothy beam. The trainer was supervising the loading of the teams soiled linen in what looked like a picnic hamper.

'Well done lads,' said the director. 'Aye, they did well,' said the manager. 'We didn't give 'em a sniff in the second half. Had the park to ourselves.'

The players had returned to their earlier clerical bracket except their hair, so soon out of the showers, was moist and springy as dewey grass.

'Didn't think I was going to score again,' said Boris, the outside right, looking back at the manager. 'That was the first for three months, And then I 'alf hit it.'

'Well as long as they go in,' said the manager. 'We're two points behind now with a game in hand. The leaders drew at Torquay.'

The bus rolled off with a snort and we had a last glimpse of silent, empty terraces covered by streaks of dancing newspaper. A group of small boys booed.

The players had changed quickly because the bus had a min line connection to catch at Crewe. Moving out of the Potteries we entered a craggy, hilly countryside. On the roadside trees wobbled hysterically in the gale and hedges puffed and heaved, exploded and crackled. The bus journey was quiet. The director discussed the good service of Kismet with the trainer and then peered out at the passing scene with half shut eyes. The manager murmured to the captain but the rest of the team hardly spoke. I noticed how, in the same way the Arsenal team had been silent and un-emotional after beating Birmingham City, in their coach, and here again was an identical atmosphere. Pleasure there was, but it was an inner one and post-mortems were non-existent. They would be left to the manager's summing up the following week. Business was temporarily over. On the train the players drank light ale and played cards.

XXVIII. Sunday Soccer

> For ninety Sunday morning minutes, sadly
> Or rarely gay, we chase the ball across
> A Lowry landscape, swearing so madly…
> MARTIN GREEN

This section will not deal with the professionals and their game, but rather with that weird bunch of London Sunday footballers who first blossomed into existence during the mid-fifties and made a stamp on the code of Association Football from which it has never really recovered.

For this I feel honoured to take some of the blame, for organizing soccer for a company of devious professional people, and others less easy to classify, who while being helplessly in love with the game, have rarely blossomed into anything more on the field than never-say-die mediocrity.

It goes without saying these days that the pastures of Hyde Park opposite Knightsbridge Barracks are littered with games involving actors, writers, poets, painters, doctors, lawyers, architects, publishers, accountants, journalists, spies, conmen, script writers, rancid layabouts, hostile Jews, cantankerous Catholics, dirty Protestants, Italian waiters, greasy Irishmen, turgid Greeks… and so on.

Our mass enthusiasm for the job is emphasized by the adroit manner in which we waggle our protruding arses as we run forward in search of the ball, by the way in which our voices rise in anger: 'You bastard. Keep your elbows down.'

Some of us look very spruce in new exotic strip with Vidal Sassonish haircuts, medallions, diamond trimmed jock straps and gold teeth. Our wives and mistresses stand on the touchline, toeing the earth like exotic mares, fluffy and uncritical and longing for this madness to end. The sides in question have strange sounding names like Chelsea Casuals, Battersea Park, Coffin Casuals, TV Scriptwriters, Cecil Gee, Soho, Primrose. We hate to lose.

Standing in Hyde Park with the sky a glorious dirty sheet of ambling black, with the rain lashing down and mud up to the ankles so that the goalkeepers have the appearance of Early Man, it is not hard to loosen a tear into the glass-tinted acres around the centre circle and say: 'Hey, hey, I was around when all this started and there were a handful of us and we didn't wear shorts because we were afraid to show our knees.' It was 1956, and Sunday soccer wasn't fashionable and actors grew fat by staying in bed until lunchtime, chipping the white froth off their tongues while waiting for the lunchtime kettle to whistle for Nescafe. This was long ago when men like Sean Connery did not hurry off to football grounds on a Sunday afternoon and join in a game far below the dreams of James Bond. When we began it was a hard grinding road in which we were faced with almost every conceivable humiliation. The beginnings were slow.

When I was finally let out of the army, in which I had only been quietly eliminated from further soccer progress after letting in thirteen goals before half-time against the Royal Horse Artillery at Aldershot, the actual chance of playing the game seemed to have finally passed me by.

There seemed no opportunity of playing the game in London. The whole network was a closed circle; a postman could play for Mount Pleasant, a printer for Reuters, a porter for Covent Garden, but for professional people I have mentioned there wasn't a game to be had and anyway the volunteers were few. Soccer was still considered the property of the working classes and should be played by them because they were the only people with talent to play it; a worthy notion.

So we grew fat and sat in pubs on Sunday mornings and talked about the game we had seen at Stamford Bridge or White Hart Lane the afternoon before. To gain exercise I wrote infuriated letters to football critics complaining of their treatment of Chelsea Football Club. Alan Ross of the *Observer* wrote back to me on one occasion: 'I know from experience that it is hard to see a team about which one feels strongly with sober eyes, but I cannot really believe you can find anything in Chelsea play to give you pleasure.'

The Royal Borough of Chelsea at that time was on the eve of a social change, which was to rip out its Bohemian guts and transform it into headquarters for the clever-clever, the zany-fashionable. It was in the Queen's Elm in the Fulham Road where I first heard that I was to be included in a team which would be playing in Hyde Park the following Sunday. In the side were a number of curios from Finch's, the Queen's Elm and the Markham Arms.

The Queen's Elm was still basically a headquarters for artists rather than footballers and actors, at that time, including John Minton, Lucien Freud, Ruskin Spear, Robert Colquhoun, Robert MacBryde, Francis Bacon, George Barker, the poet wearing a rustic goalkeeper's cap: a rumbustious moody centre. On the barstool sat the late *Daily Express* journalist, John Macadam, who was one of the few customers there who really knew the game. He was a marvelous wit and his wingy moustache bobbed up and down as he told funny stories about goalkeepers. When I told him I was actually playing football, he said: 'You'd better kick off with a rush.'

I looked forward eagerly to that game, cutting down on the lobster and gulls eggs at Claridges, offered nightly in mounds by the mothers of debutantes who wanted this roving gossip-columnist to put their names in the paper. It was a case of getting vaguely fit and the regime was ordered.

It was a regime which was not adhered to. David Stone, the novelist, who recently died, gave a memorable party in Edith Grove in which the house received excessive mutilations. The police arrived and were promptly almost disemboweled by a carnivorous painter who showed him great dexterity in knocking off their helmets. As they dragged him off in a state of exhaustion with blood spurting out of his nostrils, I asked David, who had chosen our side, if he was selected for our team. 'No,' said David, 'but I've got a Hungarian.' This was a touch of genius because the Hungarian was called Sandor and had played for a class team in Budapest; a refugee who had recently escaped during the 1956 revolution.

The next night we trailed into Finch's for a drink and met the Hungarian, a somewhat frail, pale-faced refugee, who was reeling and muttering: 'I want a woman.' I visualized him joining the SW3 mob who were forming into a clique called the Chelsea Set.

Whatever they say to the contrary, this over-glamourized set lived through days and nights of aimless boredom gate-crashing parties and hanging against the bar of Finch's and the Markham Arms, waiting and waiting for the next party, the next man or the next girl. It was easy to get into and easy to get out. This was usually done through the resources of genuine talent.

This was what fashion-designer Mary Quant had, and she actually profited from the whole mystique, making money in quantities with her King's Road shop and 'super' designs. And Samantha Eggar, with windswept, robin-redbreast coloured hair, became a Hollywood star. Others drifted back to where they had come from, to wither in the cosiness of their ancestral homes, married to pimply girls, who had decided it was time to brush their teeth.

But some of it was hilarious if you didn't let it hold you down, and some of the girls were beautiful. It was in this atmosphere that Sandor, David and I drank that evening in Finch's and Sandor let out the odd belch.

Sex, of course, was a predominant problem at that hour of night, but most available crumpet had flown and Sandor had to moon over his drinks. We felt if we didn't find him a woman he wouldn't play for us against the other mob.

The other mob was a side of Cambridge people I didn't personally know at that time. They had in fact been playing a number of weeks, a sturdy bunch of lads including a thin, handsome young Scot called Karl Miller, who had just come down from Cambridge, now literary editor of the *New States-man*, Tony White, then an Old Vic actor of distinction, now an author, and Neil Ascherson, the Bonn correspondent of the *Observer*, and Jonathan Miller, who went on 'Beyond the Fringe'.

On that first morning, during the Suez crisis, six of them and one intrepid girl went out into the park, in a sense to work off feelings of antipathy towards Eden. Six out of forty had accepted.

David eventually dragged Sandor off home, the muscular Magyar uttering mild obscenities below his breath as he tiptoed down the Fulham Road with the grace of a mating ostrich.

The next morning I woke up red-rimmed in my basement flat, with rock-n-roll cackling in my ears. 'You're playing football this morning,' said my flat mate, who had made tea for his actress girlfriend, unleashing mild squeaky snores from the next room. 'Poor bastard. What do you want to play football for?'

'Because of this,' I said, pointing to my belly. 'And besides I love the game. Got an Alka Seltzer?'

I put on my duffle coat over a pair of rugby shorts drifting below my knees and a T-shirt with moth holes on my chest and made off for the park, my football boots, Army surplus, tucked in a suit-case full of Spanish sand.

A cold, misty morning in February. As I crossed the park in the silence of a Sunday morning I became conscious of others of a similar stamp moving towards a grass strip near the Serpentine, their jeans, duffle coats, beards, hair and suit-case merged into one mass of sticky raffishness. The odd girl bursting out of her jeans walked along beside them trying to keep pace. Two players started running with a football and throwing it to each other.

'I haven't come to play that game', I said. 'That's the only game I know how to play,' said a grave intellectual named Nicholas Tomalin, who was at that time a gossip columnist on the *Daily Express.*

David appeared with Sandor in his car, staring out at our mob with mirth broadening over his face. 'We must be mad,' he said, coming over to me. 'Ah, our Honved friend has made it.' I said.

After some confusion, Karl, a whispy Burns figure, with a rich dissenting Scottish voice, and Tony, tall, enormously attractive and totally immersed in black leather, got their side, mostly players in jeans and jerseys, lined up, while David and I sorted our lot out.

By some strange twist of misunderstanding, we had thirteen a side, but that didn't seem to worry anybody. Our goal post was a grandiose, awe-inspiring tree looking like John Charles, and during their first attack, Tony's team, running forward in one solid wave, carried ball and goalkeeper and almost the tree towards the direction of Marble Arch.

From the kick-off I flicked the ball to our Hungarian inside left, and said: 'For God's sake do something.' He was still half-asleep muttering 'I want a woman' but the feeling of leather at his feet brought some sort of recollection in him of stadiums far away in Budapest, Puskas and Kocsis. He set off shaking off his randiness and after beating five prostrate men, cut towards the goal which was a pile of duffle coats, beating another five men with one flick of his waist. I was running along beside him steaming, my lungs groaning and jerking after two minutes running. There was the slapping of flesh as men who had rarely played the game before tried to tackle with their heads, backsides and necks. Sandor went past Jonathan Miller, who for some unknown reason was crouching, and still the Hungarian flew, majestically beating all and now coming up on the goalkeeper who was as big as a tank and a solid demon designer with the name Assheton Gorton; he swung his boot and crashed in a shot which was surely a goal, had I not been running vigorously towards Bayswater ahead of our champion. The shot hit me on the backside and bounced away and Sandor roared: 'You firker.'

We lost that game, although Sandor scored ten or eleven goals, but we would have surely won but for our defence.

At any rate these Sunday games were clarified as a craze and every Sunday from then on we used to meet by that John Charles tree and bash each other to pieces. As the word spread in the Chelsea pubs, more people came: con men in Bentleys and advertising men with brandy on their breath, and poets with woolen knickers as bootlaces and intellectuals on motor scooters, and one day we played with a man with one leg who came crashing through our defence on his crutches.

A few weeks later we took a team up to Cambridge to play King's College, and this time we had an even better player than Sandor, another Hungarian who was living in a house that had partly been turned over for refugees by the owner. Sandor, somewhere, had found a woman and disappeared.

The night before the match the son of that household gave a party in the main sitting room, and I was astonished to find in the jocular, boozey atmosphere, that we were surrounded by temporary beds in which a number of figures lay snoring contentedly.

The refugees had retired early, pulling off their trousers and yawning in their underpants and completely oblivious of the roar of Cambridge conversation.

The next day our Hungarian massacred the men of King's. His shooting was so strong that it drove their goalkeeper almost brutally into the goal with the ball. He dribbled at will through their defence and we stood by and let him get on with it. It was a case of giving him the ball and letting him go away contentedly like a man on horseback in Rotten Row. Sweat poured off the men of King's who bravely acknowledged defeat by a master.

But our Hungarians faded from the scene and we never saw them again. It was a time for reorganization and planning with our limited resources. About this time, Brian Glanville, author and *Sunday Times* sports writer, was introduced to me by David Sylvester, art critic, over a dirty game of table soccer. I invited Brian along to Hyde Park for our Sunday games, and he accepted with alacrity, having like me had no opportunity to play since his schooldays at Charterhouse.

Presented with the chance of playing football as a rugged left-back, Brian's fanaticism for the game broadened, his hips grew larger, his voice boomed higher, he was convinced at last that he could kick a football in the right direction.

Both of us became involved with the intricacies of park football and whether or not a tree could be beaten by sheer skill alone. Our telephone conversations analysing the game often lasted a good hour.

The name of the club was eventually suggested by David Stone, and we became Chelsea Casuals during the autumn of 1957. But dissension was already creeping into the side. On wet, ghost-like evenings we would assemble like a group of pieds noirs in a Chelsea garage, where Tony White had a temporary job.

The question was who to leave out during the organized games which were creeping into the schedule. We had acquired a number of players, including a master-baker from Swiss Cottage, an Olympian goalkeeper, an escort of Princess Alexandra, a soap-sud salesman, a Chelsea butcher's boy, a string of mysterious layabouts exuding beer and brandy breath.

These meetings became extremely tetchy with everyone disagreeing about who should play and who should be left out. An element of seriousness was creeping in and the pounding the Casuals got against the BBC at Motspur Park when Frank

Bowling, the British Guianese painter, came on gleaming at half-time in perfect strip to hammer the ball into our own net, because he still had his eyes shut after an all-night session in a night-club, told us that something would have to be done quickly.

We were annihilated by the Old Etonians on their playing fields, the referee surprising our master-baker, who prided himself at having at least played reasonable football in the R.A.F., by controlling the game with a broken leg. 'You're like a pack of hounds,' said an OE. Contemptuously. But we managed to break one of their jaws.

About this time Brian and I, through a mysterious piece of luck started training one night a week at the Queens Park Rangers ground with yet another invention which had come into being: The Showbiz XI. There the glossy stars came and the budding disc jockeys – Ronnie Carroll and Glen Mason and Andrew Ray and Ziggy Jackson, whom we called 'bearded Ziggy'.

We used to do some lapping under the astute, patient care of the Queens Park Rangers' trainer, Alex Farmer, play six asides and then take a long bath. The organizer of the showbiz team was the disc jockey Jimmy Henney, who would sit like a contented sheep dog in Mr. Farmer's treatment room being massaged on the calves. Everything then was 'fantastic'.

Those dark nights gave one the impression of a small, provincial railway station being invaded by a travelling circus full of lispy, showbiz chat. As towels were rubbed over ripe flesh, the latest jokes were recalled with howls of laughter and fat actors weighed themselves with much concern on the scales of the Third Division club.

The Showbiz team eventually were able to call on a number of former professionals and Wally Barnes, Billy Wright, and later Tommy Docherty have become almost fixtures in the set up. But in 1958 they were still in there pioneer stage, so when we met in a game at Hendon that spring it was like two primitive wagon trains running into each other.

The mud came up to our waists and the Chelsea Casuals were again annihilated by 7-1. We were soon at a disadvantage, the crowd obviously fancying the Showbiz team in their gleaming black strip against our somber, semi-laundered rags, our left-half was taken to hospital with a slipped cartilage and our inside-left was drunk, having consumed ten brandies on his way to the ground. After the game we discovered that the elaborate tea which had been laid on had been devoured by hangers on.

From then on Chelsea Casuals gradually moved out of its cocoon in the park and became deeply committed to engagement on L.C.C. pitches at Hackney Marshes, Wormwood Scrubs and Wandsworth Common, against sides with odd-sounding names – Shaftesbury Avenue Fire Station, Speedway Riders, Arsenal Supporters' Club, Western Union.

It was on these vast windy open spaces where goalposts were as numerous as gravestones in a city cemetery that we came under the harsh, hostile glare of teams who knew these pitches as well as their own palm sweats. We looked out of place in the little box huts without showers, where we were forced to change, mere shacks, in which twenty-two men and a referee were expected, for a small fee payable to the London County Council, to take their trousers down at the same time.

Brian had introduced Reg Drury to captain the side, a shrewd football writer bred on Hackney Marshes, a pencil-thin, eagle-eyed East Londoner, who viewed our inept manoeuvers with undisguised horror through glinting steel-rimmed glasses. Reg, on one occasion at Hackney Marshes, as the other team arrived without proper strip to play us, complained: 'I wouldn't mind ordinarily, Brian, but I've got friends on the Marshes.'

Brian also introduced an Italian coach, a young blonde Florentine called Piero, who tried to force us into some sort of coherent combination. Tears swelled into his huge eyes during the game as he bellowed at the fast disappearing centre-forward: 'John, don't run away.'

The selection committee, as it was, moved to my flat, but the atmosphere grew even worse. Tony White and Karl Miller had already formed a splinter group which moved to Battersea Park and became the club of that name. It was the quality of seriousness which was creeping into Chelsea Casuals which they objected to, so away they went over the river and into other mists.

In my flat we would sit huddled around my bed working out who was to play and why. Our left-half, a painter, who had introduced an element of Zen into his game, broke up one of these sessions when he had made a long speech in my defense, saying that I was not sleeping at nights because there was an undercurrent of opinion in the team insinuating that I was a natural goalkeeper, and not a natural centre-forward. 'John needs time to think about this, to achieve a peace of mind which will tolerate such brutality. His sleeplessness is due to exterior disorders. He must be allowed to achieve a balanced mind. And I want to be captain.'

There was a loud barking sound from the rest of the team as the last of the Spanish Rosè was drained, cantankerous sounds of disagreement.

Brian was right when he said these sessions were run on group therapeutic lines without the analyst. They had to stop.

So we advanced forward in disorder, although clad decently now in red strip, with the selection of the team nominally in the hands of Brian and myself, although usually before our team really caught on it took about fifty telephone calls to get a side at all.

The sickening Sunday dawns when the telephone would ring and a voice would wheeze down the other end of the line: 'I can't play today. I've got pneumonia.' 'Oh, for God's sake, why?' The groans of a wife beside one saying: 'Can't you tell your bloody muddy oafs to ring up at a reasonable hour?'

Dialing a number in Willesden for a London School of Economics student and the long wait down the other end

as one hung on for a naked bleary-eyed form to pick up
the receiver with a snort and apologise that he couldn't play
because his corns were hurting. Tracking down a student of the
Royal College of Art in Wandsworth and giving him elaborate
instructions about getting to Wormwood Scrubs and that one
would meet him at East Acton tube station at 10.15, and then
the long wait and nobody coming, and the tubes rattling by in
streaks of plunging red, and nobody coming, and Reg's long
look in the dressing room, lacing up his legs with a mile of
bandage.

And the rainy mornings ringing the ground and the L.C.C.
park keeper saying: 'It's hoff', and the delight in is voice as he
rubbed it in. The dirty teams which we sometimes took on,
such as one lot on the Fulham Sportsmen's League at Tooting
Common, who threatened the referee with violence during the
game if they lost and the referee meekly giving them a winning
goal after the right-winger had crossed the ball a good yard over
the line, so much so that he fell over in the long grass.

And the tactics of some of the dour Sunday players that
one got to know, and learnt to give back; the centre-half who
put his square skull in my mouth as I endeavoured to go past
him and I bit hard on bone and bristle and took away a good
lump as he came down on top of me and said: 'Go Easy.'
And the nigglers, the weasel-faced inside-forwards from sweet
factories and printing works who kept up an incessant: 'Ref, hey
ref, ref, hey, keep your hands down, ref, penalty ref, hey ref, you
bugger, ref, no goal, ref, offside ref.'

And the players of a Sunday morning, the tall spade at
Hackney Marshes, a temporary goalkeeper, with a blue
corduroy cap, brilliant yellow jersey, pink shorts, white socks
and new boots, smoking a fag in the goalmouth before the
game, as nonchalant as a jazz pianist between solos. A full-
back at Sandhurst saying: 'Permission to go up for a corner,
Sir' to his captain, and being refused. The inside-forward
we had transferred to us from the Royal College of Art, an

ex-Rochdale professional, who never stopped giggling when he had the ball. David Miller, of the *Sunday Telegraph*, beating three men and running on to make a telephone call. Our 'Zen' left-half going through periods of meditation during the game by making quiet tackles on non-existent opponents. Our centre-half we picked off the park, after he called us 'a bloody shower' and nicknamed 'Blondie'; a player of fickle disposition, whose sudden generosity would make us scream and Reg howl. Reg refusing to be congratulated after he had scored and muttering: 'All right, one's not enough,' Reg, who knows all the pros, pleasing a great hunk of a man called Strain in the dressing room before a match: 'I know you son, Gravesend Reserves,' and a great chest swelling out in appreciation: 'That's right, that's right.'

But confusion grew less and less and Brian fanatically bore on from year to year with almost savage seasonal programmes with over thirty games on the schedule. The Italian coach had gone, Reg was still there as captain but the side had altered shape with an experienced Scottish element woven in incorporating a fastidious quality of professionalism, a hardness of play which swung the club's formations and turned them into a winning combination, with decisive victories against all the sides who had previously humiliated us. Brian still sits at the telephone with fantastic zeal for finding fixtures, so much so that I feel he could get a team out of the Zoo for the Casuals if necessary.

The other sides who have grown into orderly groups too. It all goes with the emancipation of football, the smoothness of the new professional with his Op-Art kit rubbing off on the modest amateur. At any rate most of our rough edges have gone. The enterprising Tony White fixed up two tours of France for Battersea Park, one in Dieppe and one in Paris, which slightly flummoxed the French who perhaps expected firmer competition than they actually got, but the Battersea team, bleary-eyed, pursued a difficult task and were never disgraced although drugged by Pernod.

The teams increase, competition swells, there is a Queens Elm league. Disorder, emotion and bloodshed can never be ruled out, we play what might be called LSD soccer, a pleasure only for the participants. The drug, at any rate, has taken a firm hold in ten years, as good a way as any of staying sane some way, although outsiders think we're barmy.

Postscript

After the 1966 World Cup, John Moynihan wrote a postscript for a subsequent edition of *The Soccer Syndrome*...

There will be no forgetting that July afternoon at Wembley Stadium, when Bobby Moore lifted the Jules Rimet trophy towards the enraptured crowd, after England had beaten West Germany. Alf Ramsey's team had won the World Cup, as he always said they would; it was no longer a dream.

The competition did not produce a team as elegant as Hungary's in 1954, and Brazil's in 1958, but England, in achieving ultimate victory, displayed an admirable perseverance and collective will power. England did not really click, however, until they knocked out the stylish Portugal in the semi-final at Wembley, the evening's hero, Bobby Charlton, scoring two exquisite goals; the much criticized Nobby Stiles blotting out the deadly Eusebio, the competition's leading scorer.

The final against West Germany was a game of agony and tension; Haller put Germany ahead, Geoff Hurst headed one back, then, twelve minutes from time, Peters lashed in what seemed England's winning goal. But Weber came up with a disputed goal seconds from time, and the English players sank to their knees in despair. Their courage and strong legs saved them in extra time, Hurst finishing the afternoon with two more goals, the first bouncing down off the cross-bar, the second an emphatic thump...The game was won and Mr. Ramsey's bunch of Norberts jived with joy.

Altogether it had been a good, if not glorious, World Cup. The ageing holders, Brazil, eliminated in the qualifying games at Liverpool; Italy incredibly squashed by the North Koreans; Hungary unfortunate not to go further after beating Brazil, being knocked out by Russia in the quarter-final; and Argentina putting a bruise on the competition in the quarter-final, their captain-less side losing to England 1-0. These were some of the highlights.

Afterword

By Leo Moynihan

The Soccer Syndrome was seven-years-old when I was born, and, sitting here contemplating its 50th birthday, I realise I have always regarded the book as somewhat of an older sibling.

Like any brother or sister, I am of course very proud of it (when a writer of Brian Glanville's calibre describes Dad's work as, "The funniest, most splendidly idiosyncratic, writing about what you could call Coarse Football which has ever been achieved," the heart of course swells).

Like any younger sibling I have tried to learn from it and I often find myself opening its pages randomly, sitting back and taking in its wonderfully idiosyncratic style. The downside of that of course – and isn't this true among all brothers and sisters? – is envy. As a writer myself, that green-eyed monster is a constant companion when I flick though its chapters.

How I chuckle through clenched teeth whenever I read the book's last paragraph and how it describes Dad and his beautifully bonkers Sunday football comrades as enjoying what might be called, 'LSD football, a pleasure only for the participants'. Then there's the comparison between a burly forward called Ronnie Rooke and Ava Gardner. Look up Rooke's features and you will see why it is so funny.

Putting my own petty insecurities aside, Dad would have celebrated his first book's anniversary with gusto. Champagne and anecdotes would have flowed in equal measure, along with a proud glint that would always appear in Dad's eye when *The Syndrome* (Dad and the book's more feverish fans tended to abbreviate it) came up in conversation.

Dad kept a scrapbook dedicated to The Syndrome. Writers are a vain breed and there is no doubt that he liked to flick through the cuttings praising his work. For instance, a review in the German newspaper, *Die Zeit*, must have offered great solace in the aftermath of a telling off from a frustrated newspaper editor (or wife!) when it called his work, 'A must read,' and that one day it would, 'Assume huge historical importance,' even comparing his use of language to Dylan Thomas (an association Dad would have enjoyed for more reasons than one).

Pride though was only one of the sparks that lit that glint in his eye. I think The Syndrome, to Dad, was a portal to his past, his footballing past when the mere thought of watching his beloved Chelsea across that puddle-strewn dog-track was sheer bliss. Opening its pages was like opening a diary, and inside only the happiest memories of days, teams, players, goals and hilarity.

Not that the book (or the fact that we have republished it) should be hailed as a brochure with which to knock the modern game and its juggernaut tendencies. No, Dad never stopped loving football. In these very pages, he compares the Chelsea of his youth to a nineteenth-century Russian novel, and so the idea that it was Roman Abramovich's many Rubles that brought so much unheralded success to SW6 always tickled him. On that memorable night therefore, in Munich in 2012 when Didier Drogba's penalty won the club London's first European Cup, it was with melancholy that I lamented that Dad had died only months earlier and I could only imagine the smile that the moment would have brought to his puffy cheeks.

It is though, those years covered by the book between the war and England's triumph in 1966 that most held Dad's attention, and within those years, I think it is the game's wingers who captured his heart.

To Dad, wingers were masters. 'To watch pretty things being done by a winger is one of the chief pleasures in watching football,' he tells us in his chapter dedicated to the art. I'd say that – to Dad – wing play at its best (and wasn't it just that in those post-war years?) was like footballing foreplay. Sure, the centre-forward – tall and noble – would score the goals but that was merely the climax.

Wing play – teasing and mesmerising – was where the fun lay. The undressing of a defence by a dropped shoulder, the caress of the ball toward the bye-line. This was what Dad loved. I wonder what he would have made of today's fashions, where it is the full-backs who are asked to 'bomb-on' and provide the width. 'Bomb on'? Dad would have laughed and muttered something about the air-raids of his childhood.

It was the World Cup in England – and the hosts' triumph with a solid but wingless midfield – in the same year as The Syndrome's publication that perhaps dampened some of that joy. With hindsight though, Dad's musings on the upcoming tournament are fascinating.

When Dad writes about Bobby Moore, he recommends that the captain must not neglect his attacking prowess, saying that he: 'Can be deadly when he suddenly switches from defence.' Two assists in the World Cup final just months later suggest Dad was right.

Alf Ramsey, though, clearly didn't dwell on the assertion that England must surely play at least one winger, but as a sometime chronicler of the current national team, it was interesting to read words such as 'Fiasco' when describing certain pre-tournament performances, or the fact that journalists and fans wanted more communication from their England side. Tournament wins aside, maybe not much has changed this last half-decade!

Half a decade? The game has gone through so much but I hope readers of Dad's book will agree that its chapters remain as fresh as ever. I have many favourites. The idea of my hungover father trying to watch a 17-year-old Pele win the World Cup whilst simultaneously trying to appease a girl, so missing her fiancé, always makes me laugh; as does the Chelsea fan so adamant that he will put his head in the oven should Arsenal win the 1950 FA Cup semi-final.

Dad and I often laughed at what might have become of this besotted but oft-frustrated supporter. Indeed we once joked that maybe he followed through on his threat but only scorched his facial hair before coming to his senses and was therefore lucky enough to see the Blues win their first championship five years later, albeit with only one eyebrow.

It is these lovelorn, crazy people who have long filled vast terraces that *The Soccer Syndrome* is so dedicated to. When Dad died, Henry Winter wrote in the *Sunday Telegraph* that his skill lay in never overlooking that the game was nothing without fans. It is a notion that plenty of supporters' groups who today campaign for cheaper ticket prices adhere to, and I love that Dad almost asks a philosophical question regarding their presence.

The query is not whether the tree that falls in the wood without a witness makes a noise, but whether the striker who careers upon goal without the roar of the crowd is worthy of mention. To Dad, the answer was always an unequivocal, NO.

So, I raise a glass to those who have returned to the chapters they love most and to those lucky souls who are visiting the book for the first time. They say that when you walk through a new city, you should look up. For me, that's what *The Soccer Syndrome* does. It takes you through the wonderful streets of football's sprawling metropolis and then takes you up, above the mere pavements until you are steeple high, very much above the norm. Happy 50th to *The Soccer Syndrome*, and well done Dad. I'm so proud of you.

Leo Moynihan
September 2015

The author with Bobby Moore at the launch of the
second edition of The Soccer Syndrome in 1987.